THE CORK GUIDE

Anne Hayden was born and grew up in Cork. She has a BA in Psychology and MA in Journalism from the National University of Ireland, Galway. She now works as a freelance journalist with the *Irish Examiner*.

THE CORK GUIDE

Anne Hayden

ROBERT HALE · LONDON

ISBN 0 7090 7626 6

Robert Hale Limited
Clerkenwell House
Clerkenwell Green
London EC1R 0HT

A catalogue record for this book is available from the British Library

2 4 6 8 10 9 7 5 3 1

Printed by
St Edmundsbury Press Limited
and bound by Woolnough Bookbinding Limited

CONTENTS

ACKNOWLEDGEMENTS

My thanks go to Andrew Russell for suggesting the project to me; to my parents, Joe and Eileen, for all their support, and to the many friends who helped out with tips and recommendations, especially Ciara and Joanna who endured endless questions and offered plenty of advice.

Finally, I am most appreciative of the help given by John and Michael Hannon who read through the typescript and made some invaluable comments and suggestions.

All illustrations courtesy of Faílte Ireland Photographic Library.

INTRODUCTION

The city of Cork is built in a valley overlooked by steep hills, with the River Lee meandering through it. The famous Cork writer, Frank O'Connor, once wrote of 'the up and down of it on the hills as though it had been built on a Cork accent'. Indeed, the sing-song accent of the people of Cork reflects the landscape of the city. It all began in the seventh century when the area, then a marsh, was inhabited by St Fin Barre, the patron saint. Over the centuries Cork developed into a bustling trading port. Ireland's second city has a rich and varied history and a busy cultural and commercial life. With a population of less than quarter of a million, it has all the amenities of a big city without most of the hassle. Its compact city centre is easy to get around on foot.

A harbour town, the city has an abundance of water. Two channels of the River Lee surround the centre and the city climbs the hills on either side of the Lee. The city's coat of arms bears the words *Statio Bene Fide Carinis*, meaning 'A Safe Harbour for Ships'.

Cork isn't as obviously visually pleasing as some of its European counterparts, but is the kind of city that becomes more beautiful the more you get to know it. While there is plenty of old architecture to admire, the city's features are not neatly arranged but are, as Daniel Corkery described them in 1917, 'flung higgeldy-piggeldy together into a narrow, double-streamed, many-bridged river valley, jostled and jostling'.

Churches and grand old town houses dating back to previous centuries sit side by side with modern shopping centres and office blocks.

Cork people are famous for being fanatically proud of their citizenship, a fact that is demonstrated by their naming of their city as 'The Real Capital'. Further testament to this is the success of the 'People's Republic of Cork' t-shirts sported by locals at home and abroad. Corkonians seem to be born with an in-built belief that their city is far superior to the capital, and probably the worst insult you could throw at a Corkonian would be to mistake him or her for a Dubliner.

Nobody could accuse the natives of not being proud of their heritage either. Just look at their street names: Rory Gallagher Square after the late great guitarist, the Jack Lynch Tunnel after the former Taoiseach, and Christy Ring Park (Páirc Uí Rinn) after the legendary hurler.

Cork has been a place of learning since the seventh century. University College Cork (UCC) has about 13,000 students while a further 10,000 or so study at Cork Institute of Technology (CIT). This large student population ensures that the city stays young and vibrant and that the pubs stay packed. There is a lively arts scene, with theatre, visual art, music and film fans well catered for. Food fans will also find plenty to satisfy their palettes, while at night, the pubs and clubs are always teeming.

Designated European Capital of Culture for the year 2005, the city is in the middle of a renewal, both physically and culturally. The redevelopment and pedestrianization of the city centre along with the cleaning up of the River Lee should greatly improve the atmosphere and aesthetic quality of the city centre. In addition, the Capital of Culture year should give the city a boost, both financially and culturally, that will last long beyond 2005.

City Library

County Cork has some of the most spectacular landscape in Ireland, from the wild and rugged coastline of West Cork to the green hills and valleys a little further north. The county is dotted with picturesque fishing villages and busy market towns. Most parts of the county can be reached from the city in day trips, but those wishing to really get a feel for the area and to discover some of the hidden treasures to be found off the beaten track will want to take longer to explore.

Most visitors will make a beeline for West Cork where there are plenty of sandy beaches, rocky coves, scenic walks and attractive fishing villages. Some of the highlights include the wild ruggedness of Mizen Head, the long, sandy beaches near Clonakilty and the gorgeous fishing harbour at Schull. Watersports fans will not be left wanting, with ample opportunity for sailing, windsurfing, sea kayaking and deep sea fishing.

Further inland, the Gaeltacht (Irish-speaking) areas around the hills of Coolea offer plenty in terms of scenery and culture. There are some great walking and hiking routes around Carrantwohill and the surrounding hills. The Irish language is still alive in these areas, and there is a strong sense of heritage.

North of the city, the Blackwater Valley boasts stately homes and castles, rolling green hills and good opportunities for fresh water fishing on the unspoiled Blackwater River.

Finally, East Cork has a few good beaches and charming fishing villages as well as some top-class restaurants that are well worth a trip out of town. Highlights include the cliff-top walk in the fishing village of Ballycotton and the gourmet dining at Ballymaloe House.

Part One

CORK CITY

1 BACKGROUND AND HISTORY

The first recorded reference to Cork dates back to AD150, when the geographer Ptolemy mentioned a town called Ivuernis, which many believe was what would eventually become Cork city. Cork's recorded history dates back to the seventh century. Since then, the city has seen Viking

St Fin Barre's Cathedral at night

invaders, Anglo-Norman settlers and English colonists. It has withstood sieges, battles, fires, a famine and a war of independence.

The Irish name for Cork is **Corcaigh**, meaning 'marshy'. The city was built on a group of marshy islands around where North and South Main Streets now lie. The area was known as *Corcach Mor na Mumhan*, the Great Marsh of Munster. **St Fin Barre**, or Lochan the Fair as he was known, came from Gougane Barra, at the source of the River Lee, to Cork at its mouth in the seventh century. It is likely, however, that a large Celtic habitation had existed on the north side of the river even before then. Fin Barre founded a monastic settlement and a university near the area on which St Fin Barre's Cathedral now stands. The monastery was quite successful and as its name spread, it became an important centre for pilgrimage with people coming from all over Europe. The motto of the present-day University College Cork is *Where Fin Barre taught, let Munster learn*. According to local legend, St Fin Barre, Cork's patron saint, is buried near the present cathedral overlooked by the famous 'Goldy Angel' that sits atop the church.

In the ninth century, **Vikings** from Norway invaded and settled in the area, followed in 914 by the Danish Vikings. It is likely that the Vikings and Native Irish communities lived together in relative peace for the next couple of centuries and there is evidence that the two communities traded with each other. It has been found that, during this period, wine and salt were being imported while wool and animal hides were being exported from the city. This was the beginning of a long tradition of trading in Cork.

In 1169, the **Anglo-Normans** arrived in Ireland and began to colonize much of the country. When they made their way to Cork, the Danes and Native Irish put up a fight but were eventually defeated. In 1185, Henry II granted the city its first charter, and in 1273, the first mayor, Richard Wine, was appointed.

The Anglo-Normans built a stone wall around the old Viking settlement and developed a prosperous medieval town. Archaeological evidence suggests that the wall was rebuilt and extended at different times. It lasted for over 500 years after the Norman occupation. In fact, some of the original walls still exist underneath street level, and parts of the old wall are on display just inside Bishop Lucey Park on the Grand Parade. During this medieval period, the town walls extended from South Gate Bridge to North Gate Bridge, with North and South Main Streets as the main thoroughfare. St Patrick's Street, the Grand Parade and the South Mall were waterways until they were built upon in the eighteenth century. During medieval times, Cork was a busy and prosperous port town populated by Anglo-Norman merchants. Wool and cattle hides were among the main exports, along with wheat, oatmeal, beef, pork and butter. Archaeological excavations have revealed evidence of metal working and leather working. Despite this prosperity, however, life in the city during those times would have been very tough with overcrowding common and disease rampant.

The **Black Death** reached Cork in the mid-fourteenth century. A large fall in population followed and brought an end to this period of prosperity. During the fifteenth and sixteenth centuries, the people of Cork had to struggle against religious oppression. There was an influx of English colonists and the Protestant Church of England religion was being forced on the people. The locals rebelled against this and refused to accept the new religion, earning Cork its name as the **'rebel county'**.

It was during the sixteenth century that **Sir Walter Raleigh** lived in Cork and wrote some of his more memorable love poems to Elizabeth I who was almost three times his age at the time. The famous English poet, **Sir Edmund Spenser**, also lived in Cork during this period and wrote his *The Faerie Queene* here. Spenser lived in the Cork area for nineteen years and it is believed that he married Elizabeth Boyle at the original St Fin Barre's Cathedral in the 1590s.

In 1601, the famous **Battle of Kinsale** took place when a Spanish fleet sailed into Kinsale harbour at the request of two Irish chieftains, Red Hugh O'Donnell and Hugh O'Neill. The Spanish joined forces with the Irish to fight Queen Elizabeth's troops but were ultimately defeated. The man responsible for plantations in Ireland, Oliver Cromwell, arrived in 1649, and from then until 1683 when a Catholic, James II, became the new King of England, Corkonian Catholics lived under very strict controls. Many were expelled from the city and forced to surrender their possessions and property.

Despite these hard times for Catholics, trade continued to flourish in the city and the first bank was opened in 1680. The Huguenots settled in Cork around 1685, and contributed to the development of the city. They settled around the area where Academy Street, Paul Street and French Church Street are now. The area is known today as the **Huguenot Quarter**.

When the English Parliament objected to the ascension of James II to the throne and replaced him with the Protestant Dutch prince, William of Orange, James fled to Ireland and encouraged his supporters to rise up against William. The **Siege of Cork** took place in 1690 when some of James's army, who were welcomed by local Catholics, joined forces with local rebels to create a stronghold against William. However, William sent an army of 5,000 men to attack and regain control. After a siege which lasted several days and during which much of the city was set on fire, the vastly outnumbered rebels were forced to surrender. The period that followed was a harsh time for Irish Catholics, as William gained control of the country and introduced the Penal Laws, designed to suppress Catholicism. During this time, Catholics were not allowed to vote, were forbidden to improve their land and no education was provided for their children.

Despite this, the city continued to flourish and regained some of its prosperity during the eighteenth century. This was largely due to trading through the port, mainly in the export of butter, beef, pork and animal hides. The **Cork Butter Market** was established in 1769 and became hugely successful. Much of the city had to be rebuilt after the siege, and many of the churches and cathedrals you see today were built during this time. It was also during this century that quays were built on the waterways of the present-day St Patrick's Street (usually called Patrick Street), Grand Parade and South Mall, and towards the end of the century, these waterways were eventually filled in.

There was a large divide between rich and poor during the eighteenth century. The merchant classes were enjoying a life of relative luxury, living in large houses in the suburbs or in grand town houses in the city centre, many of which you can still see today. However, for the poor, things were very different. A large population increase in the middle of the century led to overcrowding, crime and severe poverty. The first workhouse was opened in 1747, and in the 1750s, **Nano Nagle** opened up her school to provide education, food and medicine to the poor. She also established the convent of the Presentation Sisters and will be immortalized in Cork history for the good work she carried out.

The first half of the following century saw the situation of the poor of Cork grow increasingly harsh, and an all-time low was reached in the middle of the nineteenth century with the onslaught of the **Great Potato Famine**. A potato blight spread across the country so that by 1846–7 the entire harvest failed, leading to starvation and mass emigration. In the twenty years that followed, it is estimated that over a quarter of a million people emigrated from Cork Harbour.

The later part of the century saw much of the present cityscape emerge. Many of the city's finer architectural structures were built during this time, including St Fin Barre's Cathedral and a number of new bridges such as South Gate Bridge, North Gate Bridge and St Patrick's Bridge.

The latter half of the century also saw the emergence of a growing nationalist movement, led by a Cork MP, Charles Stewart Parnell. His Nationalist Party sought home rule, but some groups wanted more independence than home rule. The Irish Republican Brotherhood (IRB) was formed towards the end of the century, a group who believed that it was necessary to use physical force to gain independence from Britain. The growing republican movement continued into the twentieth century. In 1916, the Easter Rising took place when a group of nationalist volunteers took over the General Post Office in Dublin and tried to take the city. The rising failed but it marked the beginning of the struggle for freedom.

In 1919, members of Sinn Fein set up Dail Eireann, an Irish parliament that was opposed by the British. During the following two years when the **War of Independence** took place, Cork lived up to its 'rebel' reputation. Two successive Cork lord mayors took an active part in the struggle. The first, **Tomás MacCurtain**, was murdered in 1920 in front of his wife and family. It was widely believed that he was killed by the Royal Irish Constabulary under directions from the British government. He was succeeded by **Terence McSwiney** who went on hunger strike in protest at the continuing arrest of democratically elected public representatives. He died in Brixton Prison later the same year after seventy-four days on hunger strike. As a result of considerable IRA activity in Cork city and county, the British government sent extra troops, known as the **Black and Tans**, to the area. In 1920, a large part of the city was set on fire by the infamous group. The City Hall and much of the eastern side of St Patrick's Street (the city's main street) was destroyed. In 1921, a controversial peace treaty was signed, and a bloody civil war ensued, lasting two years.

The 1920s saw industry come to Cork, most notably Ford and Dunlop. The departure of these businesses in the 1980s was responsible for an economic depression in the city as thousands of workers lost their livelihoods.

During the Second World War, the city, like many others, experienced economic decline. However, the 1960s brought investment from large chemical and engineering firms, and Cork is still very much a centre for the pharmaceutical and engineering industries. The depression of the 1980s was followed by a boom in the 1990s, and the city flourished again.

The future looks bright for Cork. A huge urban renewal project is underway in the city centre, and the Cork main drainage project, which is designed to clean up the river, is the largest environmental project in the country. It promises to make the River Lee clean enough to swim in. Also an influx of visitors and investment is expected as a result of the city being designated European Capital of Culture 2005.

Present-day Cork

At the time of writing, there is a buzz of activity about the city. Cork City Council's urban renewal plan has seen the entire length of St Patrick's Street renewed with new paving, wider footpaths, less traffic, new lighting and landscaping. The €12 million project was carried out under the guidance of Spanish architect Beth Gali who was responsible for the renewal of Barcelona for the 1992 Olympics. While the design has provoked varied reactions from

Newly pedestrianized St Patrick's Street

the public, it is surely an improvement on the shabbiness that preceded this renewal. By the end of 2005, Oliver Plunkett Street will also be renewed and will be pedestrianized from 11.00 a.m. each day.

The area around Emmett Place has also been greatly improved, with a new wing added to the Crawford Gallery, a much-needed facelift given to Cork Opera House and in front of the theatre a newly pedestrianized plaza has been laid that is used mostly by skateboarders.

The city's university (University College Cork – UCC) and institute of technology (Cork Institute of Technology – CIT) keep the city young and alive. The high number of graduates has also attracted industry and investment. Cork did not suffer as badly as many Irish towns during the dot com crash in the late 1990s as much of the employment is in the pharmaceutical and engineering sectors.

Nowadays, it is a place where people emigrate to rather than emigrate from and it is usual to hear French, Spanish and Italian accents when walking along the streets. The city has a distinct European air about it, albeit a damper air than most parts of Europe.

Crawford Art Gallery

Holy Trinity Church at Father Mathew Quay

Places to visit of historical or archaeological interest

St Patrick's Street, the Grand Parade and the South Mall

These streets in the city centre were all waterways until the Corporation decided to fill in the canals in 1780. Along the South Mall, there are still some buildings that were once reached by boats rather than cars. These buildings were specifically built to cater for storing merchandise. They usually have steps up to a large door above street level with an arch underneath where the boats used to unload goods directly into the cellars. Boats were also towed along the South Mall to their berths on the Grand Parade.

During the eighteenth century, the waterway that St Patrick's Street now covers was lined with two-storey warehouses. The ground floors of the warehouses were used by merchants to store goods, while their staff used the first floors as offices. At the Chateau bar on the corner of St Patrick's Street and Academy Street, you can see an example of the outdoor staircases that were used to reach the first floor.

Shandon

On the side of a hill on the north side of the city, Shandon is a charming area to walk around with narrow laneways offering glimpses of the city centre below. It is one of the oldest continuously inhabited areas of the city and offers a sense of the real 'old Cork'. The area's name comes from the Irish 'Sean Dún', meaning 'old fort'.

The pepper pot steeple of **St Anne's Church**, Shandon, built in 1722, is the city's most famous landmark and can be seen from

St Anne's Church, Shandon

many parts of the city centre. Two sides of the tower are limestone and the other two red sandstone. An old rhyme goes:

> *Partly-coloured like its people,*
> *Red and white stands Shandon Steeple*

It makes sense then that the Cork colours are red and white. Each side of the tower displays a clockface. The minute hands on the east and west faces skip ahead of the other faces, but synchronize again on the hour. As a result, the steeple is also known as the 'four-faced liar'. An inscription on one of the clocks reads '*Passenger, measure your time, for time is the measure of your being*'. On top of the steeple is a salmon-shaped weather vane known locally as the 'goldy fish'.

During a bout of homesickness while in Rome in the 1830s, a Cork priest, Father Mahoney, scratched on the wall of his room his poem 'The Bells', which has been inflicted on Cork schoolchildren for generations:

> *With deep affection and recollection*
> *I often think of those Shandon Bells*
> *Whose sound so wild would, in days of childhood*
> *Fling round my cradle their magic spells*

It is well worth paying the small admission fee and climbing the 100-odd steps to see the eight bells, weighing six tonnes altogether, in action. You may even get a chance to play a tune on them, and you'll get a magnificent view of the city into the bargain. For more information, call (021) 450 5906 or look up *www.shandonsteeple.com*.

Next to St Anne's Church is the **Cork Butter Market**, which was in use from the late 1700s until 1924 and was regarded as one of the most important butter markets in Europe in its day. At the height of its success, the market was exporting half a million casks of butter a year. It now houses a butter museum and craft centre. Adjacent to it is the unmistakable rotunda-shaped Firkin Crane, now used as a dance centre.

St Fin Barre's Cathedral

The French Gothic style church was built on the site where St Fin Barre is believed to have founded his monastery in the seventh century. It is probably Cork's richest piece of architecture, and its three elegant spires overlook the city. The central spire stands at 73 m, while the other two are almost 55 m tall. The cathedral was designed by William Burgess, who also designed all of the stained glass, sculptures, mosaics,

St Fin Barre's Cathedral

furniture and metal work, so that there is a remarkable unity of style. The church was made with Cork limestone on the exterior, while the inside walls are Cork red marble. The building features some fine carvings and statues. A carved doorway that is now inserted in the south boundary wall is believed to have been part of the medieval church that stood on the site long before the present-day cathedral was built. The Resurrection Angel, known locally as the 'goldy angel', stands on top of the sanctuary roof and watches over the city.

The cathedral is open Monday to Saturday 10 a.m.–5 p.m. in summer, 10 a.m.–12.45 p.m. and 2 p.m.–5 p.m. in winter. Sunday services take place at 8 a.m., 11.15 a.m. and 7 p.m. Admission is €3 outside of service times. To book a guided tour, call (021) 496 3387. Website: *www.cathedral.cork.anglican.org*.

University College Cork (UCC)

A 10-minute walk from the Grand Parade, UCC is a thriving campus which has been an integral part of Cork life over the last 150-odd years. Its population has grown considerably since it opened its doors to 115 students in 1849. The college now has over 13,000 students and seems to have taken over much of the western side of the city. Many newer buildings have sprung up around the original three-sided quadrangle. The Tudor-Gothic style quad was designed and built in local limestone by Thomas Deane, probably modelled on Oxford and Cambridge colleges. The quad is in perfect condition and still lies at the heart of the university. The Aula Maxima (great hall) is located in the north wing and is now used for music recitals and important college events. The mature gardens of UCC have a stream running through them and the campus is a pleasure to walk around. The **Honan Chapel** on the campus was built in 1916, modelled on the twelfth-century Hiberno-Romanesque style. Have a look at the nineteen stained glass windows, eleven of which were designed by Harry Clarke with the rest by Sarah Purser. A large new art gallery, the Glucksman Gallery, opened recently on the campus, and should make a trip to UCC all the more worthwhile. The university's website is *www.ucc.ie*.

Cork City Gaol

On a hillside overlooking Sundays Well, the old gaol looks more like a castle or a stately home than a prison. It was a prison from 1824 to 1927, after which it was used as a radio broadcasting centre until 1958. The building has been restored and is now open as a heritage centre. Visitors can walk in and out of the old cells, some of which are furnished with life-sized waxwork figures and sound effects. The old gaol has a fascinating history, ranging from public executions in the mid-1800s to hunger strikes in the 1920s. On a foggy day or at dusk, the place can have quite an eerie feel to it. The building also houses a radio museum, although this is less interesting. The heritage centre is open seven days a week, March–October 9.30 a.m.–5 p.m., November–February 10 a.m.–4 p.m. Admission is €5. Tel: (021) 430 5022. Website: *www.corkcitygaol.com*.

Cork Vision Centre in St Peter's Church

There has been a church on this site since 1199. In 1782, the first church was taken down and the current one was completed in 1788. After the St Peter's Church of Ireland was deconsecrated in 1949, the building was used as a storehouse until 1994 when it was renovated and re-opened as the Cork Vision Centre. This exhibition centre displays past, present and future plans for the city of Cork, and houses a large model of the city centre, scale 1:1,500. There is a useful touch screen

Cork City Gaol

information stand that was designed especially for the centre, featuring plenty of information about Cork's historical and cultural life. The centre regularly showcases visiting exhibitions, often of photographic work. To find out about forthcoming exhibitions, log on to *www.corkvisioncentre.com*. Open Tues–Sat 10 a.m.–5 p.m., admission free. Tel: (021) 427 9925.

The English Market

An indoor market was built in 1788 on the Grand Parade to sell meat, fresh fruit and vegetables. The English Market is still

The English Market

in operation today and is one of the highlights of any visit to Cork. Nowadays, the meat, fruit and veg stalls stand side by side with gourmet food sellers specializing in all sorts of olives, patés, cheeses, pastas and oriental foods. Open from 8 a.m. to 6 p.m., Monday to Saturday, the market is always teeming and is worth strolling through to take in the atmosphere and the smells as well as to admire the beautiful structure. It is not too difficult to imagine the place 200 years ago. A quality café and restaurant, the Farm Gate, is located on the upstairs balconies overlooking the nineteenth-century fountain by the Princes Street entrance (see Restaurants section). It is possible to access the market from the Grand Parade (opposite Bishop Lucey Park) from an arcade off St Patrick's Street and from Princes Street.

Red Abbey Tower

The Red Abbey Tower is the oldest piece of architecture in the city. It is all that remains of the friary that was built by the Augustinians in the thirteenth century. They arrived in Cork in 1280 and were given some land outside the city walls by the Normans. The Augustinians built a friary of red sandstone and later added the 19.5 m high squared limestone tower that you can see on Red Abbey Street, tucked away between Dunbar Street, Douglas Street and George's Quay on the south side of the river.

Cork Public Museum and Fitzgerald Park

Cork Public Museum is located inside Fitzgerald Park along the Mardyke on the western side of the city. It has a good display on Cork's role in the War of Independence and has a number of interesting archaeological exhibits. The museum is open Mon–Fri, 11 a.m.–1 p.m. and 2.15 p.m.–5 p.m. (to 6 p.m. June to August), Sunday 3 p.m. to 5 p.m. Admission is free. Tel: (021) 427

0679. Fitzgerald Park is a pleasant place to spend an hour or two on a sunny day. The gardens span an area of 18 acres and are well kept, and there is a good play area for kids. One of the prettiest parts of the park is the suspended Daly Bridge, known locally as the Shaky Bridge, which crosses the Lee to Sunday's Well. The bridge does exactly what the name says: it shakes slightly from side to side as you walk across it and is always a hit with kids.

Bishop Lucey Park, Grand Parade

This small city centre park is not the most picturesque place to spend a summer's day but is the only park right in the centre of town so on a sunny day it tends to be full of people eating lunch or chilling out. On not so sunny days, the park tends to draw a less savoury crowd. It is worth a short visit, however, to see the entrance gates which were once part of the cornmarket that stood in the nineteenth century where the City Hall stands now.

City Hall

Cobh

Just inside the gates, you can see some of the original medieval town walls, and further inside the park there is an ornate fountain that was commissioned for the city's 800th anniversary in 1985.

Queenstown Heritage Centre, Cobh

Situated 12 km from Cork city centre, Cobh (pronounced Cove) was a major departure point for many of the millions who emigrated from Ireland during and after the Great Famine that began in 1846. In the 100 years from 1846, two-and-a-half million emigrants departed from Cobh. Housed in the old Cobh railway station, an impressive heritage centre has been established to commemorate those who were forced to leave the country as a result of the potato famine. You can learn about the conditions on board the early emigrant ships, including the dreaded coffin ships. Cobh was also the last port of call of the ill-fated *Titanic* in 1912, and almost 2,000 lives were lost with the sinking of the *Lusitania* off Cork Harbour in 1915. Annie Moore was the first emigrant to be processed in Ellis Island, New York, and her story and that of her two brothers is dramatically and poignantly told. The centre offers a genealogical record-finder service, using information passenger manifests from emigrant ships that sailed from Cobh, for anyone trying to trace their Irish name or roots. Open seven days a week, 10 a.m.–6 p.m. with last admissions at 5 p.m. (closed 21 Dec–2 Jan). Admission is €5. Tel: (021) 481 3591. Website: *www.cobheritage.com*.

BASIC ORIENTATION AND INFORMATION

Cork is a compact city and is easy to get around on foot. The city centre is an island surrounded by the two branches of the River Lee. The main shopping street is the s-shaped St Patrick's Street. At the bottom of St Patrick's Street is a large statue of Fr Theobald Mathew. From here you can cross St Patrick's Bridge to Bridge Street and the north side of the city. Bridge Street leads up to the steep incline of St Patrick's Hill or around the corner to MacCurtain Street. If you walk in the opposite direction from the Fr Mathew statue, the curve of St Patrick's Street will eventually lead you on to the wider Grand Parade. Pedestrianized side streets lead off from either side of St Patrick's Street. To the right hand side of St Patrick's Street as you walk towards the Grand Parade is the Huguenot Quarter, an area full of cafés and trendy boutiques. This area encompasses the pedestrianized Paul Street, French Church Street and Carey's Lane, as well as nearby Emmett Place, on to which Cork Opera House and the Crawford Municipal Art Gallery face. On the opposite side of St Patrick's Street, pedestrianized side streets lead to Oliver Plunkett Street and then to the business area of the South Mall. The Grand Parade is a wide street that leads to another channel of the Lee. A right turn off the Grand Parade will take you on to Washington Street and out to UCC and the western side of the city. North and South Main Street, which were once the main thoroughfares, run parallel to the Grand Parade.

On the hills to the north of the city centre are the affluent suburbs of Sunday's Well and Tivoli and the less affluent

Carey's Lane

Blackpool and Mayfield. South of the river, the city spreads south towards Turner's Cross, Ballyphehane and Glasheen and sprawls west towards Bishopstown and Ballincollig. Douglas and Blackrock are to the south-east of the city.

Emergency services

The emergency services number for ambulance, fire brigade and police is 999.

The city's largest public hospital, **Cork University Hospital**, is on Wilton Road by the Wilton Roundabout (Tel: (021) 454 6400).

Anglesea Street Garda Station is the main station located behind the City Hall (Tel: (021) 452 2000). Other city centre Garda stations are located on Cornmarket Street, MacCurtain Street and Barrack Street.

There is a **Family Planning and Women's Health Clinic** on Tuckey Street that provides advice and emergency contraception if necessary (Tel: (021) 427 7906).

Money

Most banks are open Monday to Friday, 9 a.m.–4 p.m. Some stay open until 5 p.m. on Thursdays. There are branches of Allied Irish Bank, Bank of Ireland, National Irish Bank and Ulster Bank on the South Mall and scattered throughout the city centre and suburbs. ATM machines are easy to find in the centre and nearly all will accept international cards.

It is very rare to find an establishment that does not accept Visa or Mastercard; most will also accept American Express. Debit or switch cards from the UK and other countries are generally not accepted but can be used in ATM machines.

Most banks operate a bureau de change service. Foreign exchange is also available at the tourist office on Grand Parade.

Allied Irish Bank, 66 South Mall. Tel: (021) 427 6811

Bank of Ireland, 32 South Mall. Tel: (021) 427 6712

Permanent TSB, 1 Lapps Quay. Tel: (021) 427 1101

Ulster Bank, 54 South Mall. Tel: (021) 427 4418

Communications

Telephone

The international dialling code for calling Ireland is +353. The code for Cork city if calling from outside the city is 021. County Cork codes range from 021 to 029 (for example the code for Bantry is 027). If calling from abroad, the 0 is dropped, so you dial +353 21 and then the seven-digit number. To dial international numbers from Ireland, dial 00 and country code.

Coin and card-operated payphone booths are scattered around the main streets of the city centre and in lobbies of hotels, guesthouses, etc. Callcards are available in most newsagents. For long-distance calls, call shops where you make a call and pay afterwards can often work out cheaper than payphones. **Talkshop** on French Church Street is good for making such calls.

Internet cafés

Webworkhouse.com, 8A Winthrop Street. Tel: (021) 427 3090. Open twenty-four hours on Friday and Saturday, and from 8 a.m.–3 a.m. during the rest of the week.

Talkshop, French Church Street. Tel: (021) 425 4255. Open 9 a.m.–11 p.m. daily.

Internet Exchange, 10 Paul Street. Tel: (021) 425 4666. Open daily, 10 a.m.–midnight.

Cableking, 128 Oliver Plunkett Street. Tel: (021) 422 2174. Open twenty-four hours a day, seven days a week.

Wired to the World, 12A Washington Street West. Tel: (021) 427 8584. Open daily 10 a.m.–midnight.

Useful websites

Cork County Council: *www.corkcoco.ie*

Cork City Council: *www.corkcorp.ie*

Event guide: *www.whazon.com*

Humorous: *www.peoplesrepublicofcork.com*

Capital of Culture: *www.cork2005.ie*

Alternative Culture: *www.wheresmeculture.com*

Tourism: *www.corkkerry.ie*

News: *www.examiner.ie*

Newspapers

There are three daily national broadsheets: *The Irish Times*, *The Irish Examiner* and *The Irish Independent*, and one daily tabloid *The Irish Star*, although Irish versions of the English tabloids are also available. *The Irish Examiner* was originally *The Cork Examiner* and is produced and printed in Cork. While now a national newspaper, its focus is still very much on the south and it provides listings for cinema, theatre and music concerts in Cork. *The Evening Echo* is a Cork-based daily that focuses on local news and community events. *Inside Cork* is a free weekly local newspaper. UK and international newspapers are available at **Easons** on St Patrick's Street and in many newsagents.

Radio

The local commercial radio stations are **Cork 96FM** and **Red FM** which is available on 106FM. While Cork 96FM broadcasts in the city and its environs, county-wide it is called County Sound and broadcasts on 103.7FM in North Cork and on 103.3FM in West Cork. UCC's student radio station, **Cork Campus Radio**, reaches much of the city on 97.4FM. RTE Radio 1, one of the national public service radio stations, broadcasts some of its shows from Cork.

Tourist office

Cork City Tourist Office, Aras Failte, Grand Parade. Tel: (021) 425 5100. Email: info@corkkerrytourism.ie. Website: *www.corkkerry.ie*. Operated by Cork Kerry Tourism, it provides both local and national tourist information as well as maps, books and itinerary and route planning. It is possible to book accommodation through them also.

June & September:	Mon–Sat	9 a.m.–6 p.m.
July–August:	Mon–Sat	9 a.m.–7 p.m.
October–May:	Mon–Sat	9.15 a.m.–5.30 p.m.

There are also tourist offices in many county Cork towns and villages including Blarney, Bantry, Clonakilty, Glengarriff, Kinsale, Macroom, Mallow, Midleton and Skibbereen, although some are only open during the summer season.

Student travel agents

USIT, 66 Oliver Plunkett Street. Tel: (021) 427 0900.
www.usit.ie

USIT, UCC Travel, The Student Centre, University College
Cork. Tel: (021) 490 2293

SAYIT Travel, 76 Grand Parade. Tel: (021) 427 9188.
www.sayit.ie

Job hunting in Cork

If you are looking for a job in Cork, the best place to start
looking is in the local newspapers. *The Examiner* has a Money &
Jobs supplement on Fridays. The best days to look for jobs in the
classified section of *The Evening Echo* are Tuesday and Thursday.

There are a number of good websites to check out as well. If
it's part-time or short-term work you're looking for,
www.nixers.com is an excellent site. Other good jobs websites that
are regularly updated include *www.monster.ie, www.recruitireland.com*
and *www.irishjobs.ie*.

FÁS Tel: (021) 485 6200, is the state-run training and
employment authority. The Cork branch is based at
Government Buildings, Sullivan's Quay (cross over the
footbridge from the Grand Parade). FÁS runs training courses
and acts as an employment agency. Jobs and courses are usually
advertised on notice boards in the windows but to apply for
any of them, it is necessary to register with them. You must
have an Irish social security number.

There are quite a few recruitment agencies in the city, most
of whom recruit temporary, contracted and permanent office
staff. While you can fax or email them your CV, the best way

to deal with them is to call in. Here there are listed some of the bigger agencies, but for a more comprehensive list, look in the Golden Pages. Most of them advertise in the jobs sections of the local newspapers as well.

Probably the best agency for office administration jobs is **La Crème** at 85 South Main Street (Tel: (021) 2300 300). Look up *www.lacreme.ie* for current job listings. **Reed Personnel** at 91 St Patrick's Street (Tel: (021) 427 5433) are also good for finding temporary and contracted office positions.

Other well-known agencies that tend to have jobs in administration and sales and marketing as well as more technical roles are:

CPL, 5th Floor, VHI House, 70 South Mall. Tel: (021) 494 4860. *www.cpl.ie*

Fastnet Recruitment, Penrose Wharf (across the river from Jury's Inn). Tel: (021) 450 9200. *www.fastnetrecruitment.com*

Noel Recruitment, 6 Princes Street. Tel: (021) 422 2179. *www.noelrecruit.ie*

For work in restaurants and bars, your best bet is often to just walk in and talk to the manager (bring a CV!).

Getting to Cork

By air

Cork Airport is a small one-terminal airport and is very easy to negotiate. It is located only six kilometres outside the city centre and a taxi fare to the centre should not cost more than

€12. Buses run regularly to and from the bus station in the city centre. A single fare costs €3.40 and a return costs €5.50.

A number of car hire companies are represented in the Arrivals Concourse. They are:

Avis, Tel: (021) 428 1111

Budget, Tel: (021) 431 4000

Hertz, Tel: (021) 496 5849

Murrays, Tel: (021) 491 7300

National Car Rental, Tel: (021) 443 2755

All three Irish airlines fly directly into Cork Airport: **Aer Lingus** is the national carrier and flies to a wide range of destinations, although some flights to Cork will have to stopover in Dublin or Shannon. To view schedules or book online, log on to *www.aerlingus.com*. Alternatively, call 0818 365 000. Their fares are usually high, but the service is good. Low fares can often be found on their website. **Aer Árann** fly from Cork to Dublin, Bristol, Birmingham and Edinburgh. They also fly from Dublin to a number of Irish and UK destinations. You can book online at *www.aerarann.ie* or over the phone on 0818 210210 from Ireland or 0800 5872324 from the UK. The budget airline **Ryanair** flies direct from Cork to Stansted in London. If you are willing to spend a few hours in Stansted, you can get from Cork to many European destinations for a very low fare. The no frills airline is exactly what it says it is. While there are no free drinks or airplane meals, and the interior of the planes are more like the inside of a bus, Ryanair will get you to your destination on time and for very little cost. Booking is only available online at *www.ryanair.com*. Book early to make avail of the really cheap fares.

Some international airlines fly into Cork, including British

Airways. However, many visitors will have to fly via Dublin or London, especially those coming from outside Europe.

By train

All trains arrive at Kent Station on the north side of the city. From there it is an easy walk to the city centre. There is usually a queue of taxis just outside the station waiting to meet the incoming trains.

Buying tickets

Train travel in Ireland is expensive and your ticket does not guarantee you a seat. Note that there are a few different categories of ticket. A day return is sometimes cheaper if you are making a return journey in the one day. If you are making a return trip within five days, a five-day return ticket will cost you slightly less than a monthly return. Student fares are available with a valid ISIC card and travelsave stamp. For some bizarre reason, single fares generally cost only a few euro less than return fares.

The trains tend to be very busy on Friday and Sunday evenings as flocks of students return home for the weekend. Take note that if there is a major sporting event or music concert on in Dublin, such as the All Ireland Final, it may be necessary to book your ticket in advance.

Rail routes from Cork

The rail network connects Cork to Dublin, Limerick, Killarney and Rosslare as well as many stops along the way. However, to try to reach anywhere further west than Galway can be described as nothing less than an ordeal.

The train service from Dublin to Cork takes two and a half to three hours and is regular, beginning at 5.30 a.m. with the last service at 9 p.m. However, the €54.50 return fare (€58 for a monthly return) does not guarantee you a seat. A single fare costs only €3 less. At busy times, such as Friday and Sunday evenings, get there early to make sure you don't have to stand between carriages for the duration of the journey. Although overpriced, if you are pushed for time the train is probably your best option as the bus journey takes up to five hours. The service to Limerick leaves fourteen times a day and generally takes one and a half to two hours. The journey west to Killarney runs eight times a day and also takes one and a half to two hours which is faster than the bus journey which takes up to three hours.

There is no direct train route from Cork to Galway or anywhere in the north-west. To take the train to Galway from Cork, you have to take the Dublin train as far as Portarlington, change trains and then take the train coming from Dublin to Galway. This takes six to seven hours so the four-hour bus journey is really the only viable option. The same goes for getting to Mayo, Sligo and most places in the west.

To see a full route map and for timetables and fares, look at *www.irishrail.ie*. Alternatively, ring Kent Station, Cork, on (021) 450 6766 between 9 a.m. and 5.30 p.m.

By Bus

Ireland has an extensive bus service run by Bus Eireann. It's usually less expensive than the train service but can often take longer. For most destinations, bus travel is the only public transport option. There are expressway buses connecting all major towns, and local buses connect more remote areas to the towns.

Buying tickets
Usually, tickets must be bought at the ticket office in the bus station before getting on the bus. If the ticket office is closed

or there is no station, as in rural areas, it is possible to buy a ticket from the bus driver. It is also possible to buy tickets online at *www.buseireann.ie*. Student fares are available with a current ISIC card or with a valid student identity card issued by a recognized third-level college in the Republic of Ireland. Return fares offer better value.

To find out timetables and fares, log on to *www.buseireann.ie*.

By ferry

Passenger ferries to Cork arrive at Ringaskiddy, 15 km outside the city. It is possible to get to Cork by car ferry directly from Wales, England and France and via landbridge to Spain.

The ferry port at Ringaskiddy is a 20-minute drive from the city. From the ferry port exit road, turn right on to the N28, signposted Cork. You go through Ringaskiddy village and go forward at the roundabout. About 5 km on, at the next roundabout, turn right, and, after another 5 or 6 km, at the Bloomfield Interchange, take the left-hand lane (marked Airport N25). This road will bring you past the Airport Travelodge on to the Kinsale Road Roundabout. The fourth exit on this roundabout will take you right into the city centre.

Swansea Cork Ferries go directly from Cork to Swansea and Pembroke. They also offer a landbridge option, where you can take a ferry to Swansea, drive through Wales and England and take another ferry to France (Dover–Calais) or Spain (Plymouth–Santander). For reservations, call (021) 427 1166. If calling from the UK, call 01792 456116. See *www.swanseacorkferries.com*.

Brittany Ferries go from Cork to Roscoff, France, in ten to fourteen hours. Tel: (021) 427 7801 or see *www.brittanyferries.ie*.

Neither **Irish Ferries**, nor **P&O Ferries** sail from Cork. Irish Ferries have routes from Rosslare to Pembroke in Wales and to Cherbourg and Roscoff in France. They also go from Dublin to Holyhead. See *www.irishferries.ie*. P&O Ferries has a route from Rosslare to Cherbourg and from Dublin to Liverpool. See *www.poirishsea.com*.

By car

From Dublin

Dublin is 255 km from Cork and the journey time is about three and a half hours but can be more if the traffic is bad coming out of Dublin. Take the R110 out of the city and follow signposts for 'the South'. The signposts will lead you on to the N7, and at times on to the M7 Motorway. After about an hour, if you follow the signposts for Cork, you'll turn off on to the N8 which will take you through Abbeyleix, Durrow, Urlingford (halfway), Cashel, New Inn, Mitchelstown, Fermoy, Rathcormac. Cashel and Fermoy should be bypassed at some stage during 2005. When you're approaching Cork, you'll come to a large roundabout at the Dunkettle Interchange. Take the third exit and you'll arrive in Cork along the Lower Glanmire Road.

From Shannon Airport/Limerick

Shannon Airport is 128 km from Cork city and about a two-hour drive. You go through Limerick city, which is 103 km and about an hour and a half from Cork. Coming from Shannon, you no longer need to go right through Limerick city, but it can still take some time to get around it.

Coming out of Shannon Airport on the N19, follow signposts for Limerick (N18). You'll come across a number of roundabouts and the third one will bring you on to the N18. You'll drive past Bunratty Castle and on to the Ennis Road Roundabout outside Limerick city. Follow the signs for Limerick. From here, follow signposts for Cork to avoid going through Limerick city.

Eventually you will get on to the N20, and after Limerick, you'll pass through Charleville, Buttevant, Mallow, and will arrive into Cork via Blackpool on the north side of the city.

From Killarney

Killarney is 90 km from Cork and the journey takes about an hour and a half. Coming out of Killarney, follow signs for the N22 (Cork, Mallow). When you reach the Park Road Roundabout, take the third exit (N22) and at the junction with the N72, follow the signposts to Cork. You will go through Glenfisk before crossing the Cork/Kerry border and driving through Ballyvourney, Ballymakeera, Macroom and Lissardagh, after which you'll come on to a dual carriageway that will bring you on to the Bandon Road Roundabout on the western side of the city.

From Rosslare

Rosslare Harbour is 200 km from Cork and the journey should take about three hours. From the harbour, follow the All Routes signs on the N25 through Kilrane to the Rosslare Road Roundabout. At this roundabout, take the first exit, signposted Cork. At the next Ducannon Roundabout, take the second exit, and then at the New Ross Road Roundabout, take the first exit, staying on the N25. After about 20 km, you'll go through Ballynabola, then through New Ross. Here, keep following signs for Waterford (N25) about 20 km away. At Waterford, stay on the N25 following the signs for Cork. You'll go through Lemybrien, and before reaching Youghal, you'll come across four roundabouts. Take the second exit at each, and you'll bypass Youghal, going on through Killeagh, Castlemartyr, and eventually come to the Dunkettle Interchange. Here, take the N8, go forward at the roundabout, and you'll arrive into Cork along the Lower Glanmire Road.

Getting around Cork

By bus

Bus is the only mode of public transport and is certainly the cheapest way to get around the city. The standard fare is €1.10. Most buses to the suburbs go from St Patrick's Street or Parnell Place. They tend to run fairly regularly, every 15 or 20 minutes, depending on the route. For timetable information, and to find out which number bus you need, call into the ticket office at the Bus Station on Parnell Place. Take note that most bus services stop around 11 p.m.

By taxi

Metered taxis have a taxi sign on their roofs and can be hailed down. There are taxi ranks at Parnell Place and on St Patrick's Street. It's usually cheaper to call a hackney. These don't have a sign on the roof and can't be hailed. You have to call a hackney company to order one or go and wait in one of the cab ranks. Some reliable taxi companies are:

Telecabs, MacCurtain Street, Tel: (021) 450 5050

Apollo Cabs, South Main Street, Tel: (021) 427 1111

K Cabs, Barrack Street, Tel: (021) 431 1211

By car

During the daytime, it can be difficult to find parking in the city centre. On-street parking is usually 'pay and display' disc parking. You can buy parking discs from most newsagents in the city centre. They last one or two hours, depending on the area (the parking sign will tell you) and cost €1.80 each. Alternatively, there are a few multi-storey car parks where you pay before leaving. These can often be more expensive than disc parking. There are multi-storey car parks at City Hall, Roches Stores (entrance from Parnell Place), Paul Street Shopping Centre (entrance from Quay) and Grand Parade. The car park at Paul Street Shopping Centre stays open later than the others.

3 ACCOMMODATION

The accommodation in this chapter is divided into four categories: hotels, guest houses, hostels and self-catering apartments. As a general rule of thumb, most of the hotels can be categorized as expensive while the guest houses tend to fall into the mid-price range with hostels in the budget category.

While most of the hotels in Cork tend to be expensive, there are plenty of very good guest houses that cost a little less. Although the guest houses may not have the leisure centres and bars that many of the hotels have, they can often have a more personal, friendly atmosphere. There are hundreds of guest houses and B&Bs scattered around the city, and the listing here is only a sample and is by no means comprehensive. Often, the best way to decide on a guest house is through word of mouth.

There are some good quality hostels in the city for travellers on a budget. Most of these have single-room options as well as dorms and tend to offer good value for money.

Finally, self-catering apartments tend to be easier to find during summertime as some of the student accommodation is rented out to visitors. There are other self-catering options available all year round, however. For families and groups, these can often offer better value for money than hotels and guest houses.

Unless otherwise specified, it can be assumed that all accommodation listed here includes free parking facilities.

Hotels

Hayfield Manor Hotel, Perrott Avenue, College Road.
Tel: (021) 484 5900
Email: enquiries@hayfieldmanor.ie
Located directly opposite UCC, Hayfield Manor is Cork's only five-star hotel. It has an excellent reputation and is only a ten-minute walk to the city centre. The original nineteenth-century house has a new three-storey building added, and the enclosed gardens feel far removed from the activity of the nearby city centre. It has all the amenities one would expect from a five-star hotel including bar, restaurant, indoor pool, gym, sauna and outdoor jacuzzi. The price of its 83 rooms ranges from €230 to €1100.

Kingsley Hotel, Victoria Cross
Tel: (021) 480 0500
Email: resv@kingsleyhotel.com
A newly built four-star hotel, the Kingsley is located opposite the County Hall on the west side of the city about a thirty-minute walk from the city centre. The nearby Lee Fields offer a pleasant walk by the river. The modern hotel is lacking in character but is well equipped with a bar, restaurant, library, internet access in all the rooms, and a leisure centre that has a swimming pool, gym, sauna, jacuzzi and juice bar. There's even a helicopter pad outside if you need one! A single room costs €135 while a double is around €175. It is conveniently located if travelling from West Cork/Kerry.

Gresham Metropole Hotel, MacCurtain Street

Tel: (021) 450 8122

www.gresham-hotels.com

Centrally located on MacCurtain Street, the three-star
Metropole is a refurbished Victorian-style building with a good
bar, restaurant and an excellent leisure centre including a pool,
gym and sauna. It is the headquarters of the Guinness Jazz
Festival in October, so if you want to be at the centre of it all,
book well ahead. Even locals have been known to book into
the Metropole for the Jazz weekend. A single room costs €110
and double costs €140. Good weekend rates are available.

Great Southern Hotel, Cork Airport

Tel: (021) 494 7500

Email: res@corkairport-gsh.com

Part of the high-quality Great Southern Hotels group, this
modern, luxury hotel is newly built and its facilities include a
restaurant, bar, business centre, and a gym with jacuzzi and
sauna. Its location next to the airport, about 2 km outside the
city centre, is convenient for trips to Kinsale and West Cork but
is a bit far removed from the centre if it is nightlife and culture
you're after. Room prices start at €145 for room only.

Imperial Hotel, South Mall

Tel: (021) 427 4040

www.imperialhotelcork.ie

This historic hotel is located right in the heart of the city along
the South Mall. The three-star hotel has been open since 1813 and
retains much of its old-style character, although some may find it
rather stuffy. Michael Collins spent his last night here. South's Bar
is plush and often busy although the two restaurants are nothing
to write home about. Its location is perfect for shopping,
sightseeing and sampling the nightlife. Rooms cost from €94.

Jury's Cork Hotel, Western Road
Tel: (021) 427 6622
www.jurysdoyle.com
Part of the popular Jury's Group, this four-star hotel
overlooks the river on the western side of the city centre,
just before UCC. It is the largest and one of the busiest
hotels in the city, although looks somewhat dated now
compared to some of the newer hotels. Its facilities include
two bars and restaurants, swimming pool, gym, sauna, jacuzzi
and squash court as well as plenty of parking space. The hotel
is an easy walk from the Grand Parade. Room rates range
from €158 to €203.

Maryborough House Hotel, Maryborough Hill, Douglas
Tel: (021) 436 5555
Email: maryboro@indigo.ie
Perched on a hill in the suburb of Douglas, a couple of miles
south of the city centre, this converted eighteenth-century
Georgian-style mansion has been greatly modernized and
does not have the charm of an old-style hotel. However, the
four-star complex has pleasant gardens and has all the usual
facilities including a bar, restaurant, swimming pool, jacuzzi,
sauna and gym. It is conveniently located near the South Link
Road which links the south side of the city, and is not far
from Cork Airport. A single room costs €140 with a double
costing €198.

Rochestown Park Hotel, Rochestown Road, Douglas
Tel: (021) 489 0800
This luxurious hotel is located in the affluent suburb of
Rochestown. It is easily accessible from the airport and is
popular for conferences. The rooms are comfortable and well-
decorated, with cable TV, direct-dial telephone, hairdryer and

trouser press. There is a bar, restaurant and conference centre, and an excellent award-winning leisure centre with a 20 metre swimming pool, gym, sauna and Thalasso therapy centre. Room rates range from €85 per person.

Jury's Inn, Anderson's Quay
Tel: (021) 494 3000
www.jurysdoyle.com
While it does not have most of the amenities of Jury's Hotel, this cheaper version is centrally located very near the bus station and not too far from the train station. It offers good value for money. The rooms are adequate and there is a flat room rate, whether there are two or three adults or two adults and two kids. The quay on which it is located is not very well lit at night so be careful.

Guest houses

Acorn Lodge, 14 St Patrick's Hill
Tel: (021) 450 2474
www.acornhouse-cork.com
Not too far up the hill from St Patrick's Bridge, this Georgian guest house is located at the heart of the city. Its large en suite rooms have TV and telephone and cost €40 per person sharing.

Airport Lodge, Farmers Cross, Kinsale Road
Tel: (021) 431 6920
If you're arriving into the airport late at night or are flying out at the crack of dawn, the Airport Lodge offers accommodation right outside the airport gates. En suite rooms in this family-run guest house cost from €40 for a single and €50 for a double including breakfast.

Gabriel House, Summerhill, St Lukes

Tel: (021) 450 0333

This guest house is a large Georgian House not far from the train station and is also convenient if coming by car from the Dublin Road. It is perched on a hill in St Lukes, an old part of Cork on the north side of town, so most of the rooms have a view over the city. A single room with breakfast costs €39 and a double costs €60.

Garnish House, Western Road

Tel: (021) 427 5111

www.garnish.ie

One of the better of the many guest houses along Western Road, this three-star luxurious guest house opposite UCC is a short walk from the city centre. It has comfortable rooms with TV and phone, and a number of jacuzzi suites and there is an outstanding breakfast menu. Room rates range from €40–€70 for a single and €35–€60 per person sharing for a double. There is also a 50 per cent discount for kids.

Lancaster Lodge, Western Road

Tel: (021) 425 1125

www.lancasterlodge.com

This four-star guest house located next to Jury's Hotel is modern and tastefully decorated. All rooms have satellite TV, radio, two direct-dial phones and internet access. If you're willing to pay extra, the two luxury suites also have widescreen TV, hi-fi system, a king-size bed and jacuzzi. Standard rooms cost €48–€80.

Lotamore House, Tivoli

Tel: (021) 482 2344

www.lotamorehouse.com

Another four-star guest house in a large, well-preserved Georgian building on four acres of gardens overlooking the

River Lee. Lotamore House is well situated if you are driving into Cork from the Dublin Road. The comfortable rooms are tastefully done up in old-fashioned décor and have TV, telephones and hairdryers. Parents note that junior suites are also available. Room rates, which include a full Irish breakfast, start at €60 per person sharing but can be less in low season.

Redclyffe, Western Road
Tel: (021) 427 3220
This redbrick Victorian guest house across the road from UCC is good value at €45 for a single and €65 for a double including breakfast. It is well-decorated and well-located, just a short walk from the city centre.

Hostels

Kelly's Hostel, 25 Summerhill South
Tel: (021) 431 5612
Although a short walk outside the city centre, this small 20-bed hostel is bursting with personality. Each room is themed after a different Irish poet, and the walls are painted with brightly coloured murals. There is a good kitchen but breakfast is not provided. A dorm bed costs €14 and a double room costs €46.

Kinlay House, Bob & Joan's Walk, Shandon
Tel: (021) 450 8966
www.kinlayhouse.ie
Located just next to the famous Shandon Steeple, this hostel is big, bright and clean. The price includes breakfast and bed linen is provided. There is a comfortable TV room/hangout area and a well-equipped kitchen. Internet access, bike rental

Shandon by night

and laundry services are also available. There are single rooms for €35, doubles for €20 per person and dorms from €13 per person. Prices are lower in low season.

Sheila's Hostel, 3 Belgrave Place, Wellington Road
Tel: (021) 450 5562
www.sheilashostel.ie
Part of a Victorian terrace on the north side of the city, Sheila's is clean and has a relaxed, friendly vibe. It has good kitchen and laundry facilities as well as a sauna, internet access and bike rental. There are plenty of good pubs on nearby McCurtain Street and it is a short walk from St Patrick's Street. Two-bed rooms are €22 per person (€25 en suite) while 4–8 bed dorms range from €14 to €16.50 per person. Prices are a little lower in low season. Breakfast is available for a further €3.20.

An Oige Youth Hostel, 1 Redclyffe, Western Road
Tel: (021) 454 3289
Run by An Oige, the Irish Youth Hostel Association, this hostel is located on the western side of the city, near UCC. Meals, laundry service, bike rental and internet facilities are available and all rooms are en suite. Dorm rooms cost from €11 per person in low season and a single room costs €30. Breakfast is not included.

Self-catering accommodation

Dean's Hall, Crosses Green
Tel: (021) 431 2623
www.deanshall.com
Directly across the road from St Fin Barre's Cathedral, Dean's Hall has three- and five-bedroom self-catering apartments that are used as student accommodation during term-time but are rented out on a nightly or weekly basis from 14 June to 1 September. All apartments have fully equipped kitchens, direct-dial telephones and cable TV. Bed and breakfast is available. There is a coffee dock, residents' bar and a very good bistro, Proby's (Tel: (021) 431 6531), in the complex. Private parking is also available. A three-bedroom apartment costs €130 for one night and €645 for seven nights. Weekend and midweek specials are also available.

Brookfield Holiday Village, College Road
Tel: (021) 434 4032
Slightly further from the city centre, Brookfield is another student accommodation complex that is rented out during the summer. Apartment sizes range from three to seven bedrooms. All have full kitchens, TV and direct-dial phones. There is a

restaurant and also a bar in the hotel that is part of the complex. What sets this development apart from other self-catering accommodation in the city is that it has a leisure centre on site, with a 25-metre swimming pool with slide, a gym, sauna and outdoor rooftop hot tub.

Isaacs, MacCurtain Street
Tel: (021) 450 0011
Isaacs Hotel on MacCurtain Street also has self-catering apartments attached to the hotel. Only a short walk from the bus and train stations, the two- and three-bedroom apartments are well equipped with dishwasher, washing machine and tumble dryer. The apartments are ideally located with plenty of good pubs and restaurants nearby. Parking is not provided onsite but there is a 24-hour car park across the road with special rates. Prices vary according to the time of year. A two-bedroom apartment costs between €100 and €130 per night and between €455 and €555 per week, depending on the season, while a three-bedroom one costs between €155 and €175 per night and between €645 and €675 per week.

Bruach na Laoi, Union Quay
Tel: (021) 431 9772
These three star luxury two-bedroom apartments near City Hall are well appointed and centrally located. The weekly rate is €510.

Looking for somewhere to live

If you are looking for an apartment or house to rent longer term, the best place to start is the classified section of *The Evening Echo*. The best days for this are Tuesday and Thursday.

Rooms in shared apartments are also usually advertised. It might be a good idea to check the notice boards in the University and in Cork Institute of Technology.

An excellent website, *www.daft.ie*, has constantly updated rental listings. There are also a number of agencies that will help you to find an apartment. However, be wary as some of these will try to charge you a month's rent to find you an apartment. You should not have to pay anything to these agencies; it is the landlord who pays the agency to find tenants. Some househunting agencies will ask for a deposit which is refundable if they do not find you suitable accommodation.

It is normal for the landlord to ask for one month's rent in advance and one month's rent as a deposit. Even if you sign a lease, you should be entitled to get out of it by giving notice one month in advance.

4 EATING AND DRINKING

Eating out

Eating out anywhere in Ireland is an expensive business these days and Cork is no different. It is easy to pay over €60 for two main courses and a bottle of wine and you are not necessarily guaranteed a high quality. However, there are a number of places where you can get a decent meal for a lot less and a few others where the higher cost is justified. The first section lists good restaurants for formal evening meals, but many of these places serve lunch as well as dinner and will generally be a lot cheaper during the day. The second section covers daytime coffee shops/cafés and lists places where you can get a good-quality lunch and a decent cup of coffee without breaking the bank. A night's drinking in Cork is never complete without a trip to the chipper afterwards, so the third section lists some of the better takeaway chipshops. Finally, the wonderful English Market merits a section all of its own, and is a must for anyone who fancies themselves as a bit of a foodie.

Restaurants

Expensive
If you're a dedicated foodie and want to splash out, make a beeline for Seamus O'Connell's **Ivory Tower** Restaurant in

The English Market

the Exchange Buildings (upstairs) at 35 Princes Street (Tel: (021) 427 4665). Seamus is one of Cork's best-known chefs and is renowned for using fresh, organic produce. The five-course set menu is the only option and costs €50 per person but is a wonderful eating experience, and is worth a bit of a splurge. The menu changes from day-to-day; take note that the restaurant closes on Monday and Tuesday. On a par with The Ivory Tower in terms of quality and freshness is Denis Cotter's **Café Paradiso** at 16 Lancaster Quay, Western Road (Tel: (021) 427 7939). Not only is it one of the best vegetarian restaurants in the country, but simply one of the best restaurants. It is relatively expensive with main courses averaging €15 at lunchtime and around €22 at night, but it is worth splashing out for a veggie meal that will impress even the most devout carnivore. The surroundings are pleasant and the ambience relaxed. Café Paradiso also has a good selection of organic wines. For a sample of the menu, check out *www.caféparadiso.ie*. **Jacobs on the Mall** (Tel: (021) 425 1530) is an award-winning restaurant serving contemporary dishes. The surroundings are plush and the service is excellent, but the prices can be somewhat steep. **Les Gourmandises** (Tel: (021) 425 1959), owned by a French woman and her husband, really does offer the real thing if you're looking for French cuisine. From the gourmet main courses to the perfect crème caramels, proper coffee and good wine, it's a real treat.

Mid-range

The Quay Coop at 24 Sullivan's Quay (Tel: (021) 431 7026) specializes in vegetarian and vegan food, but can be somewhat bland. The restaurant is open for lunch and dinner with main courses costing around €7. There is a good-quality organic and wholefood shop downstairs. For more information, go to *www.quaycoop.com*. Built in an old bakery, **Isaacs** Restaurant at 48 MacCurtain Street (Tel: (021) 450 3805) is one of the busiest restaurants in Cork so that you are likely to find a good atmosphere even on a Monday night. They serve a wide range of fresh dishes including seafood, steaks, poultry and salads, which are reasonably priced. Behind Isaacs, **Greenes** Restaurant (Tel: (021) 455 2279) serves a similar style menu, although slightly pricier and with less atmosphere. They have a good early bird option if you arrive before 7 p.m.

Nearby on Bridge Street, **Star Anise** (Tel: (021) 455 1635) also deserves a mention for its reasonably priced, innovative dishes. It is open for lunch and dinner, except on Mondays. **Fenn's Quay** on Shear's Street (Tel: (021) 427 9527) is an intimate bistro-style spot with a simple, stylish menu. Evening main courses cost €15-20, but there is a three-course early bird option for €20 if you order before 7.30 p.m. (closed Sundays). See *www.fennsquay.ie*. **The Douglas Hide**, 63 Douglas Street (Tel: (021) 485 7463), is a pub and restaurant that blows the conventional notion of pub grub out of the water, with a delicious, simple menu that uses fresh, organic produce. The bright, spacious room is more a restaurant than a pub these days, open for lunch and dinner seven days a week, but you can pop by for a drink at the bar as well.

There are plenty of options if you are looking for some pasta or pizza and a glass of wine. **Milano** at the bottom of Oliver Plunkett Street (Tel: (021) 427 3106) serves a good selection of tasty if somewhat overpriced pizza in a modern, minimalist restaurant setting. Salads and some pasta dishes are also available. The newly opened **Pizza Republic** on South Main Street also serves good pizza as well as a wider variety of pasta dishes and some filling salads. It is reasonably priced with a good wine list. **Luigi Malones** (Tel: (021) 425 1531) in Emmett Place opposite the Opera House has a menu that stretches much further than the typical pizza and pasta dishes to include Mexican and traditional meals served in very generous portions. Main courses average €20 in the evening but there are good lunch deals and it's one of the few restaurants in the city centre that opens for Sunday lunch. See *www.luigimalones.com*. On narrow Carey's Lane (off Paul Street), **Gambieni's** serves tasty Mediterranean and Italian dishes in a lively atmosphere. **Trattoria Casanova** in the Triskel Arts Centre on Tobin Street is an authentic, atmospheric Italian restaurant, and is perfect for a meal after taking in a show or visiting an exhibition.

The options for international cuisine are more limited when it comes to Chinese, Thai or Mexican food but there are a few good-quality options for each. **Taste of Thailand** at 8 Bridge Street (Tel: (021) 450 5404) serves authentic Thai dishes in congenial surroundings. Main courses average about €15 but with the early bird option a three-course meal costs €20. **Nakon Thai** in Douglas Village (Tel: (021) 436 9900) has a good reputation for authentic Thai cuisine at reasonable prices. The menu is extensive.

For Chinese food, **The Ambassador**, 3 Cook Street (Tel: (021) 427 3261) sets the standard. It is certainly the best known and most consistent Chinese restaurant in the city. There is a set menu option that allows you to taste a wide variety of dishes. The atmosphere can be somewhat formal. **Pearl River**, on nearby Princes Street (Tel: (021) 427 4149), serves mediocre Chinese food at less expensive prices. Also on Princes Street, **Tao Tao** (Tel: (021) 425 4969) is a more contemporary take on the Chinese restaurant. The bright, minimalist décor, informal atmosphere and light, tasty dishes make a refreshing change from the traditional Chinese experience. Outside the city centre, **The Wylam** in Wilton (Tel: (021) 434 1063) is one of the better Chinese restaurants, and the **Briar Rose**, 33 Douglas Road (Tel: (021) 429 2055), also has a good reputation.

Café Mexicana on Carey's Lane (Tel: (021) 455 1241) serves decent, inexpensive Mexican fare in warm, colourful surroundings. The food isn't outstanding but is probably the best option if you have an urge for Mexican. Luigi Malones (see above) also has some good Mexican dishes on their menu.

Daytime coffee shops/cafés

While most of the restaurants listed above serve lunch as well as dinner, there are also plenty of daytime cafés that will often be less expensive for a light lunch. **Café Idaho** on Maylor Street was one of only two Cork establishments featured in the *Bridgestone Guide's Top 100 Restaurants in Ireland* (The Ivory Tower was the other). Café Idaho provides good coffee, baps and desserts at reasonable prices. Its dark wood interior provides pleasant surroundings to meet up with someone for a coffee and a chat or a light lunch and glass of wine. Open 9 a.m. to 6 p.m., Monday to Saturday. **Café Gusto** on Washington Street has some of the best coffee and sandwiches in Cork. The sleek, minimalist interior and large windows provide a great spot for people-watching but the uncomfortable seating means that you're not likely to hang around too long. You can order online at *www.cafegusto.ie*. **Les Gourmandises** serves set menu lunches and dinners with a French accent, decent coffee and wine list too. The set lunch costs €15. It reopens as a full restaurant in the evenings but is considerably more expensive.

The location alone is reason enough to have lunch in the **Farm Gate**. Housed in the English Market, the restaurant is placed on a balcony that overlooks a nineteenth-century fountain surrounded by fruit and veg stalls. Fortunately, the food is excellent too. On one side is the less expensive, self-service café which serves soup, gourmet sandwiches and luxurious cakes. On the other side is the slightly more expensive restaurant with a fuller menu, table service and a wine list. Either side is great for people-watching.

Located inside the Crawford Gallery on Emmett Place, **Ballymaloe at the Crawford** serves morning coffee and lunches to well-to-do ladies who lunch and arty types. Owned by the highly regarded Ballymaloe House, the food is fresh, local and of a consistently high standard. It also provides a much less expensive way to sample the Ballymaloe cookery.

Housed in a charming, high-ceilinged old building on Paul Street, **The Gingerbread House** serves up mediocre soup, baguettes and pizza slices but is best known for its delicious cakes and pastries. Always busy, it has a good atmosphere and is one of the few cafés that stay open until the small hours. Around the corner on French Church Street is **Amicus** (Tel: (021) 427 6455), a trendy, modern restaurant that serves breakfast, lunch and dinner. Their lunch is good value, with filling salads, wraps and pasta dishes for less than €10. When the weather's good, there are tables outside on the pedestrianized street.

Oz Cork on the Grand Parade (Tel: (021) 427 2711) has a wide-ranging lunch menu including soup, sandwiches, wraps, pasta and burgers usually for less than a tenner. In the evening the menu is more expensive, although it is the only place in town where you can order kangaroo.

Takeaway chippers

As with any city, there are the usual fast-food chains scattered about the city centre and there are plenty of chip shops that fill up as soon as the pubs close. **Lennoxes** on Barrack Street has attained legendary status in Cork for its deliciously greasy chips. Stopping off for a bag of chips on the way home from the pub is the perfect way to finish off a night on the beer. Be prepared to queue. **KCs** in Douglas Village is another spot where you can expect to queue for your pitta and chips but it is usually worth the wait. They provide the usual burgers and chips, but most locals know it's the filled pittas that cause the queues on a Friday evening. Although terribly unhealthy, if you feel like indulging in some greasy food, this is the place to be.

The English Market

The English Market, placed right in the centre of the city, is a joy to stroll through, a feast for the senses. With stalls selling everything from fresh fish and meat to stuffed olives and organic fruit and veg, it is a food-lover's paradise. There are three entrances, one on the Grand Parade, one on Princes

Street and one on to St Patrick's Street. Some of the highlights include **The Real Olive Company** which sells all sorts of stuffed, fresh olives and **On the Pigs Back** which is famous for its chicken liver pâté and which also sells delicious cheeses and cold meats. **Iago's** specializes in fresh pasta, sauces and cheeses and also sells great coffee while the **Alternative Bread Company** has a mind-boggling variety of homemade breads. The **Central Coffee** stall has some of the best coffee in Cork. There are also plenty of fruit and veg sellers, fresh fish vendors and butchers. It has to be one of the highlights of any trip to Cork. For more information on the English Market, see the Places to Visit section.

Tipping

It is customary to tip when you receive table service in restaurants, usually about ten per cent of the bill. Most restaurants pay their waiting staff a minimum wage on the understanding that the staff will receive enough in tips to make up the difference. If you receive particularly good service, you may wish to tip more than this, but by the same token, if you feel the service is not up to scratch, do not feel obliged to leave anything. It is usually better to leave tips in cash, as credit card tips do not always get to the waiting staff.

You will not be expected to tip in places where there is counter service. If there is a tip jar on the counter, it is up to your own discretion whether or not a tip is merited. Many people will throw their change into the jar.

It is not customary to tip bar staff unless there is table service. However, some people will tell the person behind the bar to 'keep the change' or 'have one for yourself as well' if they find the service friendly.

Pubs and bars

Cork seems to have been taken over by modern superpubs in recent years, but there are still plenty of cosy, friendly pubs in which to wile away a few hours. Plenty of the large, modern bars and the smaller cosier pubs serve food during the day and often have live music or DJs in the evenings.

Ireland's licensing laws mean that pubs close at 11.30 p.m. on weeknights and at 12.30 a.m. on Friday and Saturday. On Sundays, last call is at 11 p.m. with half an hour 'drinking up time'. There are a few bars that have late licences, meaning they can serve until 2 a.m. Once the rest of the pubs close, these places tend to fill up very quickly. Nightclubs also stay open until 2 a.m. but almost always have an admission charge. There are also a few early houses which have a harbour licence allowing them to open at 7 a.m. (except on Sundays) in case you feel the urge to keep on going from the night before.

As in most places, weekend nights are busiest. Don't expect to find a seat easily after 9 or 10 p.m. on a Friday or Saturday night. The larger bars will often have more people standing than sitting. Generally, during the week, the pubs still tend to be busy (largely due to Cork's large student population) without being uncomfortable.

It can be very difficult to get a cab once the pubs close on Saturday nights. It is not wise to walk around the city alone at this stage of the night either, as people fall out of the pubs and the chip shops, when fights or scuffles are not uncommon.

Live music bars

Located next door to City Hall, **The Lobby Bar** is Cork's best-known live music venue. The upstairs area consists of a small bar and an even smaller stage. Despite the fact that it is often packed, the sound is excellent and it is a very enjoyable and intimate gig venue. There is free live music in the downstairs bar on most nights of the week as well. The Lobby tends to have a full programme of events, generally of a high quality, from Irish and international acts. For more information, log on to *www.lobby.ie*. Like The Lobby, **An Spailpín Fánach** on South Main Street has a pub downstairs and a small live music venue upstairs. Traditional Irish music sessions (trad sessions) are frequent in the main pub while young local bands often take over the upstairs venue. Look out for open mic nights as well.

A small pub bursting with atmosphere, **Sin É** (meaning 'that's it' and located next to a funeral home) on Coburg Street is an ideal place to spend a winter afternoon with a pint and the newspaper, or to spend an evening chatting with friends. The walls and ceilings are covered in posters, fliers, postcards and old concert tickets. There is a small room upstairs which often plays host to live music at night. Trad sessions regularly take place downstairs also. Next door to Sin É, **The Corner House** regularly plays host to trad sessions and live gigs. The pub tends to have a lively, friendly atmosphere and is always busy.

Fred Zeppelins on Douglas Street is where many local bands play to their first live audience. Popular with indie and rock/metal fans, as well as a few bikers.

Music bars (with DJs)

The Bodega on Cornmarket Steet was the first of Cork's trendy superbars and is still by far the most tasteful. Built in a beautifully renovated old warehouse, the bright open space with high ceilings, rafters and whitewashed walls is a lovely spot for coffee during the afternoon and for drinking in the evening. The large white walls usually showcase art pieces from local talent. DJs play most nights of the week and it is open late at the weekends. At the weekends, there is a club in the White Rooms upstairs. The admission charge is usually about a fiver but if you just want a couple of late pints, you can stay in the main bar until late on Friday and Saturdays. The lunch menu isn't bad and brunch is served until 4 p.m. at the weekends. Nearby, **The Rhino Rooms** on Castle Street draws a similar crowd to the Bodega. It's a one-up, one-down trendy bar that used to be known as the Roundy House due to its semi-circular exterior. The minimalist interior does not take from the warm atmosphere, although it can seem a little pretentious. There are DJs several nights a week.

Cleavers on Liberty Street is another newly opened bar with the leather seating and minimalist décor that seems to be becoming the standard for new, 'trendy' bars. However, this small bar tends to have more atmosphere than most of the trendy spots and usually has good music too. It used to be a butcher's shop (hence the name). Around the corner on South Main Street is **The Classic** which also has DJs playing most nights of the week. The interior is decorated with old movie posters. The tables by the big windows at the front provide seating for those who want 'to be seen' and there tend to be plenty of those.

Cosy pubs where you can get a decent pint of stout

Tom Barrys on Barrack Street is a gem of a pub that serves pints with a smile. Perfect in the winter for a cosy pint by the fireplace with a decent beer garden for those rare sunny days. Decorated with fairy lights, candles and local artwork, this is one of the friendliest and cosiest spots in Cork. They even put photocopies of the *Irish Times* crossword on the tables in case you need something to occupy your mind. Live music every

Thursday. Also on Barrack Street, **The Gateway**'s claim to fame is that it's the oldest pub in Cork and maybe Ireland. Popular with a studenty crowd, it tends to be busy every night of the week but rarely gets so packed that it's uncomfortable.

The Hi B is tucked away upstairs on the corner of Oliver Plunkett Street and Winthrop Street (entrance on Oliver Plunkett Street side). A Cork institution, the Hi B looks more like someone's living-room than a pub, and like a pretty small living-room at that. It is always filled with colourful characters. The owner is renowned for his intolerance to mobile phones. They are strictly banned and he will have no qualms about kicking you out if he sees you chatting on one. A piano in the corner is regularly put to use and there is a large music collection behind the bar, mostly classical. Around the corner on Winthrop Street, **The Long Valley** is another local institution. A pub steeped in literary tradition and local history, you'll always find good conversation, good pints and decent sandwiches too.

Hidden away in a little lane off St Patrick's Street (near the entrance to the English Market), **The Mutton Lane Inn** has been a popular drinking spot for many years. Dark, smoky, candlelit and full of atmosphere, it has recently been taken over by the owner of Sin É, another of the most atmospheric pubs in the city.

Dennehy's on Cornmarket Street is another old pub that is always teeming; its popularity is owed as much to the friendliness of its proprietors as it is to its relaxed atmosphere. It provides the perfect antidote to the 'trendiness' of the Bodega across the road.

Foreign beers/microbrews

The Franciscan Well on the North Mall is a microbrewery and pub with an impressive beer garden at the back. Local microbrews such as Blarney Blonde and Rebel Red are the order of the day. The brews are tasty but very strong – a few of these could have you flying for the night. The pub holds a very popular Oktoberfest during the October bank holiday weekend each year when a number of different brewing companies set up shop in a marquee out the back. The beer menu in **Abbots Ale House**, 17 Devonshire Street, is certainly more extensive than any other pub in Cork. It's a great place to try out different types of foreign beers or local microbrews in a relaxed pub setting.

Gay bars

The gay and lesbian scene in Cork is fairly limited. However, while there are only a few 'gay bars' as such, there are plenty more in which gay couples can feel comfortable.

Loafers at 26 Douglas Street is Cork's oldest and best-known gay bar. It's a friendly and relaxed drinking spot, whether you're gay or straight, and has a nice beer garden out the back as well. **Taboo** on Faulkner's Lane (off St Patrick's Street) is a newer, smaller but more flamboyant bar which regularly features cabaret and drag shows, karaoke and live DJs. **The Other Place**, 8 Augustine Street (off North Main Street), houses a café, a bookshop specializing in gay and lesbian literature, and also serves as a gay nightclub at weekends.

Late bars

There are a number of late bars that stay open until 2 a.m. each night. When the rest of the pubs close at 11.30 or 12.30, these bars fill up and regularly have queues outside. **An Bróg** on Oliver Plunkett Street is an indie music pub that is open until 2 every night of the week and is always full of students and indie kids. If you like dark, noisy, grungy pubs with atmosphere and aren't fussy about waiting for your pints, this is the place for you. However, if you fancy getting dressed up and having a few sophisticated cocktails, keep well away.

Scotts on Caroline Street serves a better-heeled crowd, mostly young professionals, although by 2 in the morning, it is difficult to tell the scruffy students from the yuppies. Loud chart music is the order of the day. The surroundings are modern, full of silver railings and neon lights. The place is a bit calmer in the early evening when there are regular jazz gigs, and is a popular lunch spot.

The enormous late bar **Reardens** on Washington Street always has people queuing out the door at the weekends. Playing chart music, it caters for shirted twenty- and thirty-somethings. The place lacks character but always draws a crowd. Havana Brown's nightclub at the back caters for a similar crowd.

Early houses

Early houses can be fascinating if sometimes depressing places, with an assortment of shipmen, twenty-four-hour party people winding down their night, night-shift workers on their way home, and respectable businessmen in for a sneaky pint before work.

The best-known of Cork's early houses is **Charlie's** on Union Quay. Charlie's tends to be busy whether it's seven in the morning or seven in the evening. Nightshift workers mix with late night/early morning revellers and hardened sailors in the early hours of the morning. Live gigs and trad sessions regularly take place in the evenings. **The Idle Hour** is a bit more out of the way than Charlie's, located right on the docks, and serves pints to sailors and dockers from 7 a.m. It is an interesting place to spend an afternoon, friendly and full of local characters.

Ship in the city docks

SMOKING

The Irish government has implemented a ban on smoking in the workplace, including all restaurants and cafés. The law took effect in March 2004. If a restaurant has outside seating, smoking is permitted in that area.

HAPPY HOURS

The happy hour is also a thing of the past as the government has also banned happy hours and cheap drinks promotions in an effort to curb binge drinking.

Clubs

In the 1990s, Cork was known as the clubbing capital, mostly because of the (in)famous Sir Henry's, known as a legendary venue to dedicated clubbers. Sir Henry's was most famous for its Saturday residency, Sweat, which ran for thirteen years, and its residents, Greg Dowling and Shane Johnson, played host to many world-class DJs over that time. While Henry's shut its doors in 2003, some new clubbing venues have opened up around Cork to ensure that local clubbers are not left out in the cold.

Some nightclubs will open all week, catering for the large student population, but apart from them, clubbing in Cork is mainly a weekend pursuit. There are several clubs in the city, some that are designed specifically for music fans, others that have vague music policies and serve as little more than late night drinking/pick-up spots (often referred to as 'meat markets').

The door policy varies from club to club. While some may not let you in if you're wearing trainers, the door policy in most clubs is pretty relaxed. The music policy also varies widely from club to club and from night to night. Admission prices are always cheaper during the week than at weekends. Generally, Saturday is the most expensive night, and guest DJs/live acts will usually cost more also. Clubs don't usually open until 11ish and tend to fill up after the pubs close. They can serve alcohol until 2 a.m. and most end at that time, but some will keep the music going for an hour or so after the bar closes.

Specific clubnights tend to change regularly so the easiest way to find out what's on during any particular night is to look out for fliers and posters or pick up a copy of *Whazon* or *Cork Life*, free publications available in cafés, shops and bars around town. A good website for listings is the clubbing section of *www.entertainment.ie*.

The **Savoy Theatre** reopened just in time for the Cork 2005 festivities after being closed for over a year due to problems with the licence. The 1,000-capacity venue is used as a live venue and a nightclub, and often as both at the same time. Converted from an old cinema, the several levels allow for different types of music in different areas. The dance floor is huge and the large capacity means it is one of the few places that can cater for well-known international bands and DJs.

At the back of the Opera House, the **Half Moon Theatre** (Tel: (021) 427 1168) opens as a nightclub from Thursdays to Sundays. The main room is a tall, black box overlooked by a balcony and hosts good-quality local and sometimes international DJs, while a small, low-ceilinged room downstairs has live bands. For event listings, see *www.halfmoontheatre.ie*.

Club One on Phoenix Street (across the road from the GPO) is one of the newer clubs and one of the few to stay open seven days a week. Its music policy tends to centre around r 'n' b and funk; the crowd tends to be quite young. Log on to *www.onecork.com*. **City Limits** on Coburg Street (Tel: (021) 450 1206) is probably best known for its comedy club that takes place every Saturday and Sunday night. It's also not a bad spot for dancing at the weekends, whether you've been to the comedy gig or not: *www.thecomedyclub.ie*. On weekend nights, the **Bodega** on Cornmarket Street (Tel: (021) 427 2878) opens up its back rooms as a club and charges a small admission fee. You can still drink in the main bar without paying in.

The **Redroom**, 17 Liberty Street, and **Club FX** on Wood Street (off Mardyke Street) are not far from UCC and cater largely for students. Their music policies are fairly vague, mostly chart music, although on certain nights there may be something more adventurous. **Vibes** on Carey's Lane is little more than a multi-mirrored meat market.

![5] ARTS AND ENTERTAINMENT

Theatre

While Cork has a relatively strong theatre presence, its profile in the visual arts has always been stronger. However, the city does have several theatre venues of varying size and several high-profile theatre companies. There is usually a decent choice for theatre-goers, and often the smaller venues are where you'll find more novel and interesting plays and shows.

The Midsummer Festival, which runs for three weeks in June, offers a broad variety of new and innovative theatre in a wide range of theatre spaces. A Fringe Festival also takes place in February.

Theatre venues

Cork Opera House, Emmett Place, Cork
Tel: (021) 427 0022
Cork Opera House is the largest theatre in the city with a seating capacity of 1000. The Opera House has recently received a much-needed facelift in time for the 'Capital of Culture' year. The all-glass façade is a vast improvement on the older version, and the two bars overlooking the River Lee have also been renovated. However, the theatre itself did not get the renewal it deserves, and can still look somewhat shabby.

As well as straight theatre, the Opera House regularly plays

Cork Opera House

host to live music events as well as the obligatory Christmas pantomimes. It serves as a vital centre during the annual Choral Festival, the Cork Film Festival and the Guinness Jazz Festival.

For a full programme of upcoming events, log on to *www.corkoperahouse.ie*.

Half Moon Theatre, Half Moon Street

Tel: (021) 427 1160

Email: info@halfmoontheatre.ie

Housed at the back of the Opera House, the Half Moon Theatre tends to be used as a club and live music venue more than as a theatre space these days. However, it does still showcase plays from time to time, especially during the festivals. It is a small black box with a small stage but the high ceiling creates a sense of space. Seating consists of rows of chairs brought in temporarily so it is not the most comfortable place to watch a play. However, it offers a welcome alternative to the more standard venues and often features more left-of-field shows. For more information on events at the Half Moon, see *www.halfmoontheatre.ie*.

Everyman Palace Theatre, MacCurtain Street

Tel: (021) 450 1673

Email: palacepress@eircom.net

The Everyman Palace Theatre, known to most as simply 'The Everyman', is worth a visit if only to see its beautifully restored interior. The Victorian theatre is a listed building. However, there is usually more than just the interior to entice you to pay a visit. With a seating capacity of 630, it plays host to a wide variety of theatre productions as well as to occasional live music concerts, often featuring less mainstream bands or artists.

To find out what's on there, have a look at *www.everymanpalace.com*. Also keep an eye out for fliers around town advertising their current programme.

Everyman Palace Theatre

UCC Granary Theatre, Mardyke

Tel: (021) 490 4275

Email: granary@ucc.ie

The Granary is owned by University College Cork and regularly shows new and experimental work by artists in theatre, dance, performance and live art. It also showcases work from UCC Drama and Theatre Studies students and from local student groups. The adaptable and intimate theatre space comprises a floorspace as the stage, with tiered seating on three sides.

Triskel Arts Centre, Tobin Street, off Grand Parade

Tel: (021) 427 2022

The Triskel, hidden away in a small alleyway off the Grand Parade, is an invaluable asset to the arts scene in Cork. The centre houses a 100-seater theatre as well as a gallery space, a workshop and a bar/restaurant. Their varied programme features drama, film, visual art, literature and education workshops. Free quarterly programmes of events are available from the centre or in many restaurants/bars in the city centre.

Firkin Crane Dance Centre, Shandon

Tel: (021) 450 7487

Located next to Shandon Tower, the rotunda-shaped building was first opened in 1855, and after being destroyed in the 1970s, was restored in the 1980s. It now houses the Institute for Choreography and Dance and provides a centre for performance, research and education.

Theatre festivals in Cork

Cork Midsummer Festival

This broad-scale festival runs for three weeks in June and encompasses a number of art forms with a particular focus on theatre, but also including literature, poetry and music. The standard tends to be high and the festival often showcases young, up-and-coming talent as well as more established names. Over the last few years, the festival has always included a major piece of outdoor street theatre.

The **Fringe Festival** takes place around January or February and focuses on contemporary, cutting-edge and left-of-field theatre.

The **Arts Festival** in November is generally a good time for theatre fans.

Local theatre companies

Corcadorca Theatre Company

The Cork-based theatre group Corcadorca is highly respected nationwide and is renowned in particular for staging theatre pieces in non-theatre venues. Previous works have included a version of 'A Midsummer Night's Dream' played out across Fitzgerald's Park and a play of 'The Trial of Christ' carried out through the city centre ending up on St Patrick's Hill. Corcadorca is also responsible for producing the award-winning play 'Disco Pigs', set in Cork, which was later made into a feature film.

Meridian Theatre Company

This company produces new and little-known work often with a local theme. Meridian has a particular commitment to music theatre so their work often features music or videos. The pieces are usually premiered in Cork and often go on to tour nationally and internationally.

Graffiti Theatre Company

Graffiti specializes in educational theatre for young people. Although based in Cork, the company tours the country bringing high-quality theatre aimed at specific age groups to schools and other venues nationwide.

Cinema

Cork people love to go to the cinema and there is a strong film tradition in the city. It plays host to the annual Cork Film Festival, which is internationally acclaimed. There are several multiplex cinemas as well as an excellent arthouse cinema, Kino. Arthouse films are also shown regularly at the Triskel Arts Centre. This isn't bad for a city this size. Most of the cinema timetables are available in *The Irish Examiner* and *The Evening Echo* newspapers. Some of the cinemas have their own websites. Otherwise, *www.entertainment.ie* is a good website to find listings for all cinemas in the city.

Mainstream cinema

The multiplex cinemas tend to show mostly blockbuster-style movies. The large number of screens does not always mean a wider choice as when major blockbuster movies are released, they will often be shown on two or more screens within the one multiplex. However, most of these cinemas also show one or two smaller-budget films and Irish productions. The Capitol Cineplex is older and shabbier than the others but has tended recently to show occasional, more left-of-field, films filling a much-needed gap between blockbuster and arthouse venues. For timetables, see *The Irish Examiner* or *The Evening Echo*.

The Gate, North Main Street
The six-screen multiplex is in a very central location and has comfortable seating and Dolby Digital Surround Sound. For credit card bookings call (021) 427 9595 and for timetable information, log on to *www.corkcinemas.com*.

The Capitol Cineplex, Grand Parade

This six-screen cinema was Cork's first multiplex and is showing the signs of age. However, it sometimes offers a more eclectic choice than the string of big-budget Hollywood fodder that fills the other multiplexes. For credit card bookings call (021) 427 8777. Timetables are available on *www.filminfo.net*.

Cinemaworld, Douglas

If you are staying near Douglas or Rochestown or anywhere on the southside of the city, the six-screen Cinemaworld is easily accessible with plenty of parking space. To book, call (021) 489 5959. Timetables are listed in the local papers and on *www.corkcinemas.com*.

The Reel Picture, Ballincollig

The Reel Picture is handily located if you are staying west of the city or near the airport. Its six screens showcase a similar selection of movies to the Gate and Cinemaworld. Call (021) 487 6300.

Note: There is a large multi-screen, state-of-the-art cinema complex planned for the Mahon Point Shopping Centre Development which was not yet built at time of going to print. It is likely that the Capitol Cineplex in the city centre will be closed down when this development is opened.

Arthouse

Kino, Washington Street
Tel: (021) 427 1571
Email: kinocinema@indigo.ie

Kino is the only independent arthouse cinema in Ireland and is an invaluable asset to filmgoers in Cork. The 188-seater cinema shows high-quality English and foreign-language films seven days a week and serves half-decent coffee instead of the usual popcorn and mineral combo. As there is only one screen showing two or three films a week, films often tend to come in and out quickly. A visit is a must for any real film fan. The Kino schedule does not appear in the local newspapers but is available online at *www.kinocinema.net* and look out for flyers advertising current shows also.

Cinematek at the Triskel, Tobin Street, off South Mall
Tel: (021) 427 2022
Email: triskel@iol.ie
The Triskel Arts Centre occasionally shows arthouse films and documentaries of a high standard. It's an enjoyable place to watch a film and then to discuss it in the bar afterwards. To find out what's showing, log on to *www.triskelartscentre.com* or look out for the programme of events brochure in shops and cafés about town.

Cork Film Festival

Usually held in the second week of October, Cork Film Festival will celebrate its fiftieth anniversary in 2005. It runs for one full week, and is undoubtedly the highlight of the year for any self-respecting film fan. Despite the fact that long-time sponsors, Murphy's, pulled out after 2001, the festival is still going strong and continues to draw filmmakers, producers and fans from all over the world. Held in a number of venues throughout the city, including Cork Opera House (a fantastic setting in which to watch a film), the Kino and the Triskel Arts Centre, the festival showcases a variety of national and international feature-length and short films. The opening and closing galas held in the Opera House tend to book out early, as do the Irish shorts. The festival prides itself on promoting the production of short films, with many different categories of short films and several short film awards.

Cork Film Centre, 20–21 Anglesea Street
Tel: (021) 431 6033
A non-profit organization supported by the Arts Council and
Cork Corporation, the Cork Film Centre aims to develop and
promote people working in film or animation. The centre
provides short courses and workshops and has a wide range of
film equipment available for hire. To find out about upcoming
workshops and events, log on to *www.corkfilmcentre.com*.

Visual art

The visual arts scene in Cork was recently given a boost by the
announcement of the planned opening of a new gallery at UCC.
According to the university's president, the Glucksman Gallery
will 'underpin the relationship between the university and the
cultural life in the region'. It is hoped that the 2,300 square
metres of gallery space will breathe new life into the area.

The Crawford School of Art and Design, now part of Cork
Institute of Technology, has been open since 1849 and has
continued to keep the city's galleries fresh and alive. In addition
to the renowned Crawford Municipal Art Gallery, there are a
number of smaller galleries and arts centres that showcase local
and international work of a high standard. An annual Art Trail
festival takes place each November when all the city's artists'
studios are opened to the public.

Galleries

Crawford Municipal Art Gallery, Emmett Place
The Crawford is one of the leading art galleries in Ireland and
is at the heart of the art scene in Cork. The older part of the
red-brick building was built in 1724, and was used as the

customs house until 1818. It became a school of design in 1850, although the Crawford College of Art and Design is now located away from the gallery by St Fin Barre's Cathedral. The

Crawford Art Gallery

eighteenth-century building was extended in 1884; the façade facing on to Emmett Place is the older part. In 2002, a competition was held to design the new extension that was to be added on to house the temporary exhibitions that are run continuously. The winning entry was designed by Dutch architect, Erick van Egaraat. His modern wing is a fine example of how to combine the old and the new without devaluing either. The permanent collection includes works by Jack B. Yeats, Harry Clarke, Paul Henry, Sean Keating and William Crozier, to name but a few. Stop to take in the stained glass window by James Scanlon, which was commissioned in 1993 and forms the centrepiece of the gallery. The continuing programme of temporary exhibitions features both Irish and international art and the gallery has even played host to works by Picasso in recent years. Open Mon-Sat, 10 a.m.-5 p.m. Admission is free. Tel: (021) 427 3377. Website: *www.crawfordartgallery.com*.

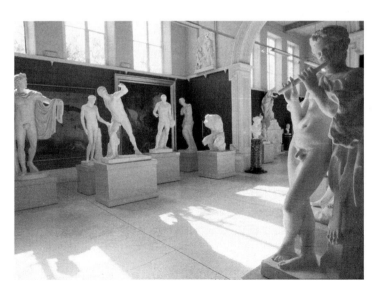

Interior of Crawford Art Gallery

Triskel Arts Centre, Tobin Street (off Grand Parade)
This centre houses two galleries, artists' studios and an intimate auditorium. The multi-purpose arts space features a varied programme that includes drama, film, visual art, literature and education workshops. Free quarterly programmes of events are available from the centre or in many restaurants/bars in the city centre. Tel: (021) 427 2022. Website: *www.triskelartscentre.com*.

Fenton Gallery, Wandesford Quay
The 2000 square feet of the Fenton Gallery seems even bigger as large windows create a sense of space and let in plenty of natural light. This successful commercial gallery regularly hosts high-quality exhibitions of painting, sculpture, prints and ceramics. There is also a beautiful sculpture courtyard that is open during the summer. Tel: (021) 431 5294. Website: *www.artireland.net*.

Lavit Gallery, 5 Father Mathew Street
A small space run by Cork Arts Society, a non-profit organization, the Lavit gallery prides itself on promoting artists' work and encouraging the development of emerging artists. The gallery sponsors the Student of the Year Award for the most promising graduate from the Crawford College of Art & Design each year. The downstairs gallery shows a continuously changing selection of traditional and contemporary work from local and international artists while the upstairs space hosts about twenty different exhibitions each year. Open Tuesday–Saturday, 10.30 a.m. – 6 p.m. Tel: (021) 427 7490. Website: *www.thelavitgallery.com*.

The Vanguard Gallery, Carey's Lane
Upstairs in a building on the charming Carey's Lane, the

Vanguard is a well-known commercial gallery space that features mostly contemporary art. Tel: (021) 427 8718.

Cork Vision Centre, North Main Street

Run by Cork Civic Trust, this beautifully restored eighteenth-century church now serves as a public exhibition centre. The centre regularly holds temporary exhibitions, often photographic, on a variety of subjects. In addition, there is a large model of Cork city that is worth a look if you need to find your bearings. The restored vaulted ceilings add to the charm and sense of space in this bright centre. The staff members are helpful too. Open Tuesday-Saturday, 10 a.m.-5 p.m. Admission is free.

Tigh Fili, MacCurtain Street

The multi-purpose centre that is Tigh Fili is one of the strongholds of the artistic community in Cork. The tall, brightly lit gallery space regularly exhibits the work of local talent, including paintings, prints, sculptures and performance art. There is an atmospheric café that serves wholesome food and artists' studios are available to rent. The centre holds courses in art and creative writing, is home to Cork Women's Poetry Circle, and publishes *The Cork Literary Review*. Not bad for a building that was once a bakery. Open Monday-Friday, 9 a.m.-5 p.m. Tel: (021) 450 9274.

Glucksman Gallery, UCC

The Glucksman Gallery opened towards the end of 2004 on the grounds of UCC. The wonderfully designed building is worth a visit to view the architecture alone but the exhibitions so far have also made an impression. While at UCC, art enthusiasts should also take a look inside the Honan Chapel on campus where you will find stained glass windows designed by Harry Clarke and Sarah Purser.

Glucksman Gallery

Crawford School of Art

The Crawford School of Art was first established in 1849, and for many years was located in the Crawford Gallery on Emmett Place. It has since moved to the old Customs House building on Sharman Crawford Street near St Fin Barre's Cathedral. The college offers five areas of study in fine art and provides the backbone to the thriving art scene in the city. Every June, the college puts on a graduate exhibition to showcase the work of that year's graduating students. It usually takes place across a number of venues including the college itself and can be a great opportunity to pick up work by upcoming artists for good prices and to support local talent at the same time. Tel: (021) 432 6445. Website: *www.cit.ie*.

Art Trail

The Art Trail is an annual visual arts festival that usually takes place around the end of November/beginning of December. For a period of two weeks, all Cork's artists' studios are open to the public and additional exhibitions and installations are put in place.

There are usually exhibitions and events in some non-gallery spaces as well as in the usual venue. In addition to workshops and talks, there tends to be at least one open submission event. For more information, call (021) 496 1449 or look at *www.arttrail.ie*.

Artists groups/studios

National Sculpture Factory, Albert Road

The National Sculpture Factory was set up in 1989 to provide artists with a large studio space and access to equipment that would not normally be available in an average studio. Housed in a large nineteenth-century redbrick warehouse, the Factory is jointly funded by the Arts Council of Ireland and Cork City Council. It is an invaluable asset to the visual arts in Cork. Tel: (021) 431 4353. Website: *www.nationalsculpturefactory.com*.

Wandesford Quay Studios

The studios at Wandesford Quay, near the Fenton Gallery, are home to the renowned Backwater Artists Group and to the Cork Print Makers. Both have a strong reputation in the city.

Cork Arts Collective

Set up in 1985 to address the needs of local artists, Cork Arts Collective is based in the grounds of St Fin Barre's Cathedral, where the group provide studio facilities including a darkroom, computer suite and reference. They organize forums, exhibitions and exchanges and aim to encourage artistic innovation and production.

Music

There is a strong musical tradition in Cork, from the traditional music that has been passed down through generations and that can still be heard in pubs all over the city to the rock music tradition inspired by the legendary Cork guitarist Rory Gallagher. The world-renowned Guinness Jazz Festival has been taking place annually for over quarter of a century, while the International Choral Festival attracts visitors from all over the globe. There are plenty of young, up-and-coming bands and singer/songwriters on the circuit, while the city's record shops are full of aspiring DJs trawling through the vinyl. Buskers usually tend to stick to the pedestrianized areas around Paul Street and Winthrop Street.

For specialist record shops, see the Music section in chapter 6.

Music festivals

The **Cork Guinness Jazz Festival** takes place on the October bank holiday weekend (the last weekend in October). It is certainly the busiest weekend of the year as the city is invaded by thousands of jazz fans and musicians. Most of the action takes place in the Metropole Hotel, which is the festival headquarters, and in the Cork Opera House. There are events taking place citywide, however. In previous years, the festival has seen the likes of Ella Fitzgerald, Dizzy Gillespie and Terry Callier take to the stage. For booking information, call (021) 429 8979 or email corkjazz@corkcity.ie. The official website is *www.corkjazzfestival.com*.

The **Cork International Choral Festival** celebrated its fiftieth anniversary in 2004. It usually takes place on the May bank holiday weekend (the first weekend of May). The City Hall is used as the main venue for recitals. The Fleishmann International Trophy Competition is one of the top choral competitions in Europe and attracts international choirs from all over the world. To find out more, call (021) 484 7277 or look up *www.corkchoral.ie*.

City Hall

There is also the **Beamish Cork Folk Festival** that takes place in early September and usually brings a couple of hundred singers, musicians and entertainers to town. It takes place in a number of different venues across the city including the Imperial Hotel, the Lobby Bar, An Spailpín Fánach and The Corner House. For programme information, contact Willie Hammond on (021) 431 7271.

Where to hear live music

There are plenty of places to hear live music around the city. Theatre venues such as **Cork Opera House,** the **Everyman Palace** and the **Triskel Arts Centre** occasionally put on live music concerts, which are usually seated. The 1000-capacity Savoy is probably the biggest indoor venue in the city, and regularly puts on live international acts. The **Half Moon**

Everyman Palace Theatre

Club also brings over acts from abroad and showcases Irish bands and artists as well.

The upstairs of the **Lobby Bar** can only hold 100 people but is still renowned as one of the premier live music venues in the country. There are gigs on most nights of the week, some for free, some with an admission charge. For more popular gigs, it is often necessary to buy tickets in advance.

A number of other pubs put on gigs, mostly from young local bands or lesser-known national acts. These include **An Spailpín Fánach** (upstairs) on South Main Street, **Nancy Spains** on Barrack Street and **Fred Zeppelins** on Parliament Street.

Traditional music can be heard for free in pubs such as **An Spailpín Fánach** (downstairs), **Sin É** and **The Corner House**, both on Coburg Street and **Aoife Landers** on Oliver Plunkett Street.

Outside the city, some of the best-known spots for live music are **DeBarra's Folk Club** in Clonakilty, **Connolly's of Leap** and **The Blackbird** in Ballycotton.

Classical recitals

The Cork Choral Society holds recitals every Thursday at the **Aula Maxima** in UCC. During the summer months, the **Crawford Art Gallery** holds a series of recitals. Occasionally, events are held at **St Fin Barre's Cathedral** and the **Honan Chapel** in UCC. Large-scale classical events such as the National Symphony Orchestra tend to be held at **City Hall**.

Outside the city, the **West Cork Chamber Music Festival** is held at Bantry House over ten days in July. The festival draws soloists and quartets from all over Europe and beyond. See *www.westcorkmusic.ie*.

During July and August, a classical music festival takes place in **St Barrahane's Church**, Castletownshend.

Literary Cork

Considering that Cork has been a centre for learning for over a thousand years, it is not surprising that the city has a strong literary tradition in both the English and Irish languages. The poet **Edmund Spenser** lived in north Cork for nineteen years and is believed to have married at St Fin Barre's Cathedral in the 1590s. He wrote his famous work *The Faerie Queene* in Cork.

In 1773, in the very different world of the Irish-speaking lands of west Cork, **Eibhlín Dubh ní Chonaill** wrote the famous 'Caoineadh Airt Uí Laoghaire' (Lament for Art O'Leary) after her husband was killed for refusing to sell his horse to a Protestant named Morris. The Irish language poem is still widely acknowledged as a masterpiece and was translated into English by Frank O'Connor.

It was during the last century, however, that Cork really flourished as a literary centre. **Daniel Corkery**'s Cork novel, *The Threshold of Quiet*, was published in 1916, followed by his *Hidden Ireland* (1927). While he may have begun a literary movement, it was his pupils, Frank O'Connor and Seán Ó Faoláin, who nurtured it to adulthood.

Cork's most famous literary figure has to be **Frank O'Connor** (1903-1966). Brought up in a poor inner city family, he was largely self-educated, but Daniel Corkery encouraged him to read voraciously and O'Connor went on to become one of Ireland's most acclaimed writers. He published two novels but it is for his short stories that he is best known. The Frank O'Connor International Festival of the Short Story began in 2000 and now takes place every year.

Seán Ó Faoláin (1900–1991) was one of Ireland's most influential novelists. While studying at UCC, he became a member of the Irish Volunteers and fought in the War of Independence. It was during this time that he began to write novels and short stories which received much critical acclaim. He also edited the literary journal *The Bell* from 1940 to 1946 and wrote biographies and travel books. His autobiography *Vive Moi!* was published in 1971 and provides an insight into Cork life.

Around the time that O'Connor and Ó Faoláin were writing in Cork city, **Elizabeth Bowen** (1899–1973), whose family home was Bowen's Court near Kildorrery in north Cork, was also coming into her own as one of Ireland's most respected fiction writers. She wrote short stories and novels. Some of her best-known works include her novels, *The Death of the Heart* (1938) and *The Heat of the Day* (1949), and her autobiographical work *Bowen's Court* (1942) set in north county Cork.

Seán Ó Riordáin (1916-1977) has been credited with being the most important Irish language poet of the last two hundred years. A poet and essayist, he lived in Cork all his life and influenced many of Ireland's leading Irish language poets in his time lecturing at UCC. **Louis de Paor** is one such poet. Born and bred in the Bishopstown area of Cork city, he is one of the country's best-known poets and writes in both the Irish and English languages. He currently resides in Galway where he is writer in residence at the university there.

Michael Davitt is another successful Cork-born Irish language poet who won the Butler prize for literature in 1994. He is a member of Aosdana, an affiliation of artists, membership of which is limited to 200 living artists who are selected by peer nomination and election.

John Montague was born in New York in 1929 and grew up in county Tyrone, but moved to Cork in the early 1970s and lived there for many years. He has published a large volume of work, mostly poetry, and has taught at UCC since the 1970s. He is widely recognized as one of the most important Irish poets of the last century, and has influenced a number of contemporary Irish poets.

Montague taught Waterford-born **Seán Dunne** at UCC. Dunne was a columnist with *The Cork Examiner* and established himself as one of Ireland's most prominent contemporary poets until he died in 1995 before he'd reached the age of forty. His books include *Against the Storm, In My Father's House* and his memoir, *The Road to Silence*.

A contemporary of Dunne, **Theo Dorgan** also studied at UCC under the guidance of Sean Lucy and John Montague and his poetry collections published to date include *The*

Ordinary House of Love, Rosa Mundi and *Sappho's Daughter*. He is a member of Aosdana, as is Patrick Galvin.

Patrick Galvin's memoirs *The Raggy Boy Trilogy* have been in the limelight recently, as one of the books has been made into a film, *Song for a Raggy Boy*. Starring Aidan Quinn, the film was shot in Ballyvourney, Co. Cork. Galvin is a well-known playwright and poet, one of his best-known poems being 'The Madwoman of Cork'.

Conal Creedon published his collection of short stories, *Pancho and Lefty Ride Out*, in 1995, and followed it with his impressive début novel, *Passion Play*, which has been an international success despite the fact that it is written in a strong Cork accent.

The contemporary literature scene of Cork is not confined to male writers though. **Roz Cowman** is an award-winning poet who lectures in Women's Studies at UCC. Her poems and reviews have been published in a number of anthologies, and her first major collection, *The Goose Herd*, was published in 1989.

Mary Leland has published novels, short story collections and non-fiction books as well as having contributed to many of the national newspapers. Her book *The Lie of the Land: Journeys through Literary Cork* is a must for anyone with an interest in Cork's literary history.

To find out more about Cork's literary heritage, call at the **Munster Literature Centre**, Tigh Litriochta, 26 Sullivan's Quay, Cork. As well as hosting the **Frank O'Connor Short Story Festival**, the centre also hosts **Éigse na gCúige** in February. It is a broad-based literary festival that focuses on a particular European regional literary tradition each year. The centre also published *Southword*, a bi-annual literary journal.

Tigh Filí on MacCurtain Street is home to Cork Women's Poetry Circle and publishes the *Cork Literary Review*. Regular readings are held in the café/art space that is housed in an old bakery. Readings are also held at the Triskel Arts Centre and occasionally at UCC.

For information on bookshops, see Chapter 6.

Festival calendar

January
Cork Fringe Theatre Festival
Across a number of theatre venues, the fringe festival focuses on contemporary and cutting edge theatre.

February
Éigse na gCúige
Organized by the Munster Literature Centre, this broad-based literary festival focuses on a particular European regional literary tradition each year. For more information, contact the Munster Literature Centre at 26 Sullivan's Quay. Tel: (021) 431 2955.

May
Cork International Choral Festival
This 50-year-old festival usually takes place on the May bank holiday weekend (the first weekend of May) and attracts international choirs from all over the world. To find out more, Tel: (021) 484 7277 or look up *www.corkchoral.ie*.

Intermedia
The multi-media event is organized by the Triskel Arts Centre and explores a variety of art forms including film, visual art and sound.

June
Cork Midsummer Festival
This broad-scale festival takes place over three weeks and encompasses a number of art forms with a particular focus on theatre, but also including literature, poetry and music. Over the last few years, the festival has always included a major piece of outdoor street theatre.

September
Beamish Cork Folk Festival
It takes place around the beginning of September in a number of different venues across the city including the Imperial Hotel, the Lobby Bar, An Spailpín Fánach and The Corner House. For programme information, contact Willie Hammond on (021) 431 7271.

October
Guinness Jazz Festival
The Cork Guinness Jazz Festival takes place on the October bank holiday weekend (the last weekend in October). It is certainly the busiest weekend of the year as the city is invaded by thousands of jazz fans and musicians. Most of the action takes place in the Metropole Hotel, which is the festival headquarters and in Cork Opera House. For booking information, Tel: (021) 429 8979. The official website is *www.corkjazzfestival.com*.

Cork Film Festival
Usually held in the second week of October, Cork Film Festival will celebrate its fiftieth anniversary in 2005. It runs for one full week, and is undoubtedly the highlight of the year for any self-respecting film fan. The festival showcases a variety of

national and international feature-length and short films. For more information, Tel: (021) 427 1711 or log on to *www.corkfilmfest.org*.

November
Artsfest
A weeklong festival organized by Cork Institute of Technology, Artsfest features music, drama and literature. Much of the action takes place on the CIT campus in Bishopstown but other venues in the city centre are also put to use.

Art Trail
The Art Trail is an annual visual arts festival that usually takes place around the end of November and beginning of December. For a period of two weeks, all Cork's artists' studios are open to the public and additional exhibitions and installations are put in place. There are usually exhibitions and events in some non-gallery spaces as well as in the usual venue. In addition to workshops and talks, there tend to be at least one open submission event. For more information, call (021) 496 1449 or look at *www.arttrail.ie*.

Year of Culture

Cork has been designated European Capital of Culture for 2005. The prestigious title is given to a city from a different European country each year and Cork had to compete with Limerick, Galway and Waterford for the title. It is a once in a generation opportunity and Ireland will not be eligible again until 2031 so it's a pretty big event.

About 140 events are planned to take place throughout the year, and about 70 per cent of those events have emerged from the public following an 'open call' for ideas and suggestions. A full programme of events is available from the Cork 2005: European Capital of Culture offices (Tel: (021) 455 2005) or online at *www.cork2005.ie*.

The events are wide-ranging, encompassing art, drama, music and literature as well as community and sporting events. Below are what should be some of the highlights: The **Relocations** series, led by local theatre group Corcadorca, will involve five months of outdoor theatre events from different parts of Europe. The **50th Cork Film Festival** will take place during 2005 and will include outdoor screenings of the world's 100 best short films. The world-renowned **Kronos Quartet** from San Francisco will perform at St Fin Barre's Cathedral. The **Oceans to City Rowing Race** will see rowing boats from all over Ireland and from abroad competing in a race from the coast right into the city centre.

The **Eighteen Turns Pavilion** is an arts space designed by Daniel Libeskind, the architect who designed the buildings that will replace the World Trade Center in New York.

The cultural scene in the city has received an economic and morale boost from winning the title, and 2005 should see an influx of visitors and a strong flow of creativity in Cork. The renovation of the city centre is due to be finished in time for the Capital of Culture year. This urban renewal project has included the pedestrianization of much of the city centre as well as a major facelift to Cork Opera House and an extension to the Crawford Municipal Art Gallery. A new visual arts centre has also been opened at University College Cork.

6 **SHOPPING**

Shopping in the city centre

The city's main shopping area is along St Patrick's Street and the streets to either side of it. There are a few shopping centres (malls) around this area. The Merchant's Quay Shopping Centre at the bottom of St Patrick's Street has quite a few clothes shops and department stores, while the Paul Street Shopping Centre has a large Tesco supermarket and a few smaller shops. There are, of course, plenty of large shopping centres in the suburbs.

Clothes

St Patrick's Street has a number of department stores such as *Dunnes Stores, Roches Stores* and the more exclusive *Brown Thomas*. Branches of many UK fashion outlets, such as *Warehouse, Oasis, Top Shop* (inside Roches Stores), *River Island, Karen Millen* and *French Connection*, can be found on the street. *Quills*, next to the Savoy Shopping Centre on St Patrick's Street, sells handknit sweaters as well as fashion. For bargains, have a look in *Penneys*. Along French Church Street, there are a few trendy boutiques such as *Le Soul, DV8* and *Store*, while *Prime Time* on Washington Street kits out the skateboarders and clubbers of Cork. *Hale Bopp* on Paul Street sells fashionable, retro second-hand clothing. For upmarket clothing and formal evening wear, try *The Dressing Room* on Emmett Place and *Sheena's* on Lower Oliver Plunkett Street.

Music

All the usual chain stores such as *Virgin, HMV* and *Golden Discs* can be found on St Patrick's Street. There are also a number of smaller specialist stores. The first floor of *Vibes and Scribes* on Bridge Street sells a good selection of new and second-hand CDs and has a small selection of used vinyl. *Plugd* on Washington Street is a gem of a store, selling an excellent selection of up-to-date indie, house, hip-hop and electronica on CD and vinyl. A few doors down, *The Vinyl Room* has plenty of house records.

Pro Musica on Oliver Plunkett Street sells brass, woodwind, string, percussion and pianos as well as accessories and music sheets. On Parnell Place, *Jeffers Music Co* also sells a wide range of instruments, as does nearby *Russells Music*.

On MacCurtain Street, *The Living Tradition* caters for trad and folk fans, while across the road, *Crowley's Music Centre* sells musical instruments and accessories, and *The Guitar Shop* sells, well, guitars.

Books

Waterstones on St Patrick's Street probably has the widest selection of books. *Easons* on St Patrick's Street has a good selection of books and stationery and has the widest range of magazines and newspapers. *The Cork Bookshop* on Carey's Lane has a good selection and helpful staff. *Liam Ruiséal* on Oliver Plunkett Street specializes in school books but also has a good sections on local history and Irish literature.

Vibes and Scribes on Bridge Street has plenty of second-hand and discount books. Other second-hand bookstores include *Connolly's Bookshop* on Rory Gallagher Square and *Good Yarns* in the Market Parade (off St Patrick's Street). *Mainly Murder* on Paul Street sells mainly murder mysteries.

Gifts/souvenirs

For some Irish-made pottery, try *Meadows & Byrne* on French Church Street or *Marble and Lemon* on Emmett Place. *Yesterdays* on Carey's Lane has some lovely old-fashioned gift ideas. Try the Shandon Craft Centre for some locally made ceramics or stained glass. *Quills* on St Patrick's Street sells handmade knitwear, as does *Blarney Woollen Mills* in Blarney. *Silver Moon* on Oliver Plunkett Street and *Equinox* on Carey's Lane both specialize in handmade jewellery with a modern twist. The more traditional *Keane's* is probably the best known jewellers in the city.

Miscellaneous

Other Realms on Carey's Lane is heaven for comic fans.

Cork Art Supplies at 26–28 Princes Street stocks a good range of artists' materials.

Maher's Coffee on Oliver Plunkett Street sells a good variety of fresh coffee beans.

Shopping centres outside the city centre

There are two large shopping centres in Douglas: *Douglas Village Shopping Centre* and *Douglas Court*. On the western side of the city, *Wilton Shopping Centre* is located opposite Cork University Hospital, while further out is *Bishopstown S.C.* The most convenient for the north side of the city is *Blackpool Shopping Centre*. Each of these shopping centres has a large supermarket and plenty of parking spaces.

7 SPORTING CORK

Sports fans won't be bored in Cork, whether it's watching or playing that interests you. There are ample opportunities to watch a football, hurling or rugby match, or to make a night of it and place a few bets on the dogs. There are good facilities for swimming and golfing, while the rugged coastline offers great opportunities for watersports enthusiasts.

Spectator sport

Gaelic games

The GAA (Gaelic Athletic Association) was founded in 1884 to encourage the playing of the native games – hurling, camogie and Gaelic football – instead of rugby or soccer. Every county, city, town, village and parish has its own GAA team and facilities, and the rivalry and tribalism is a major feature of any GAA match. If you're not from Ireland, one thing you should definitely do is go to a hurling or Gaelic football match. For each sport, each county has its own team that competes in an All-Ireland competition each year. Cork's team are known as The Rebels and can be easily identified by their red and white kit.

Páirc Uí Chaoimh is the main stadium in Cork and is

used for big matches, for example for county finals and All-Ireland matches. To get to 'the park' as it is known, take the number 2 bus from Parnell Place and get out at Ballintemple. The first left turn after the bus stop will bring you to the stadium. The smaller **Páirc Uí Rinn** is used for less important games. Good floodlight facilities mean that matches sometimes take place after dark here. Take the same bus route, but when you get out at Ballintemple, turn right and walk up Temple Hill. When you get to the top, Páirc Uí Rinn is directly across the road.

Rugby

Rugby is a very popular sport in Cork, with a number of rugby-playing schools and high-profile clubs such as **Cork Constitution, Dolphin** and **UCC**. Rugby matches can occasionally be seen at Musgrave Park or at Cork Constitution.

Munster has been at the forefront of European rugby for many years now and the team has beaten both the Australian Wallabies and New Zealand All Blacks. Their supporters are famous for their dedication and knowledge of the game. If you are lucky, you may see them play in **Musgrave Park**, although they tend to field their more high-profile matches at Thomond Park in Limerick – their spiritual home.

Soccer

Cork City Football Club is based in Turner's Cross. The team is one of the top teams in the country's amateur premier league and has a huge support base of vocal fans. For info on results and upcoming fixtures, look up *www.corkcityfc.ie*.

Horse racing

Cork Racecourse just outside Mallow is the premier venue for horse racing in county Cork. It was completely refurbished a few years ago. Admission is usually about €15, and a race card costs €2.50. Corporate packages and suites are also available. To find out fixtures and times, look up *www.corkracecourse.ie* or Tel: (022) 50210.

Greyhound racing

The newly built dog track at Curraheen Park Greyhound Stadium in Bishopstown is a popular venue for a night out. The complex has a bar and a restaurant, The Laurels, so you can place a few bets on the greyhound races over a few drinks or dinner. The park is open Wednesday, Thursday and Saturday nights, with ten races per night, the first one starting at 7.50 p.m. Admission is €7 midweek and €8 at weekends. Tel: (021) 454 3095.

Participatory sport

Golfing

There are a number of golf clubs of varying quality in and around the city, including a championship course. Here are listed some of the better quality courses.

Cork Golf Club at Little Island (Tel: (021) 435 3451) was designed by the famous golf course architect, Alastair McKenzie. Overlooking Cork Harbour, it has changed little in almost one hundred years, but is a fascinating test of golfing skill. Green fees cost €80 midweek and €90 at weekends (fees are lower for groups). Check out *www.corkgolfclub.ie*.

About 10 kilometres outside the city, **Fota Island Golf**

Club (Tel: (021) 488 3700) is a championship course which
has hosted the Murphy's Irish Open as well as the Irish PGA
Championship. It is quite expensive with green fees from €62
to €98 depending on the day of the week and the season.
Caddy hire is available. See *www.fotaisland.com*.

By far the most exclusive golf course, the **Old Head Golf
Links** at Kinsale (Tel: (021) 477 8444) caused a lot of
controversy when it was being built a few years ago as it is placed
on a magnificent cliff top that has been a popular scenic walk for
centuries. It is certainly one of the most magnificent settings
imaginable for a golf course. A 'heli-golf' option is even available,

Golfing on the Old Head of Kinsale

where golfers are transported to the course via helicopter. Green fees cost from €250 and the course is open from mid-April til the end of October, 7 a.m.–11 p.m. *www.oldheadgolflinks.com*.

Douglas Golf Club (Tel: (021) 436 2055) is much more accessible with green fees costing around €50. In the easily accessible suburb of Douglas, this flat course is relatively scenic despite its city location. The club is open from 8 a.m. to sunset. See *www.douglasgolfclub.ie*.

Swimming pools and leisure centres

There are plenty of leisure centres with gyms around the city, some of them with swimming pools as well. However, most of them operate on a membership-only basis, so unless you are staying in Cork for more than a few months, your options are limited.

UCC Mardyke Sports Complex on Mardyke Road (about 10 minutes walk from the city centre) is only open to members.

Leisureworld in Bishoptown (Tel: (021) 434 6505) is a City Council-owned leisure centre located next to Cork Institute of Technology. It comprises a six-lane 25-metre swimming pool as well as a gym and steam room. Open Mon, Wed, Fri 7 a.m.–10.30 p.m., every other day 9 a.m.–10.30 p.m. Admission to the pool costs €5.50 before 3.45 p.m., €7 after. Admission to the gym is €7.

Leisureplex on MacCurtain Street (Tel: (021) 450 5155) has ten pin bowling, pool tables and plenty of arcade games. It is open twenty-four hours.

Hillwalking

Hillwalkers at **Union Chandlery** (Tel: (021) 455 4334) at 4–5 Penrose Quay next to the bus station is the best place in the city to go for hiking gear and for information about hillwalking. Hiking gear is also available from **The Great Outdoors** on Paul Street.

There are loads of fantastic spots for hillwalking all over county Cork. See the West Cork section for info on the **Beara Way** walking route, and the North Cork section for info on the **Blackwater Way** route.

Equestrian

The best place for those interested in horse riding to start out is **Hop Island Equestrian Centre** near Rochestown. The centre has floodlit indoor and outdoor arenas and offers lessons, forest treks and beach rides. To get there, follow the road to Rochestown, and after you pass the Rochestown Inn, take a right turn. Tel: (021) 436 1277.

Water sports

Cork is ideally located for water sports fans. Whether it's sailing, windsurfing or canoeing you're into, there's plenty of coastline to play around with. Just be sure to wear a wetsuit!

A good place to start is **Oyster Haven Activity Centre** (Tel: (021) 477 0738) which is a 20-minute drive from the city. The centre offers beginner, intermediate and advanced courses in windsurfing and sailing. If you do not wish to take a course, you can hire windsurfing boards or canoes and wetsuits.

For sailing fans, the **Royal Cork Yacht Club** at Crosshaven (Tel: (021) 483 1023) and Kinsale Yacht Club (Tel: (021) 477 2916) offer marina facilities to visitors. Sailing courses at all levels are available at Oysterhaven Holiday and Activity Centre and at **Kinsale Outdoor Education Centre** (Tel: (021) 477 2896). **International Sailing and Powerboating** (Tel: (021)

481 1237) at East Beach, Cobh, has been run by Eddie English for over thirty years. He provides sailing lessons, windsurfing lessons and equipment and has a good website at *www.sailcork.com*. If you're going further afield, it is possible to do sailing courses in Baltimore, Schull and Adrigole (see West Cork section for more details).

Surfing is becoming increasingly popular in Ireland, and there are a number of good spots around the Cork coastline, including Garrettstown, Inchydoney, Castlefreke and Barleycove. There is a surf shop, **Incide**, on Bridge Street and another, **Tubes**, inside Matthews on Paul Street. The staff at either of these shops will give information on where to go.

Other activities

Actionpak Outdoors and Activities (Tel: (021) 477 6050) organize paintballing outings and specialize in event management. They are based in Ballyregan near Kinsale and will organize transport if requested. **Kinsale Outdoor Education Centre** (Tel: (021) 477 2896) organize sailing, windsurfing, canoeing, rock climbing and powerboating.

Bookmakers

The most widely spread bookmakers are Paddy Power's and Ladbrokes, both of which have several branches across the city and county. Both also cater for online betting at *www.paddypower.com* and *www.ladbrokes.com*. In the city centre you'll find **Ladbrokes** on Marlborough Street, Barrack Street and Parnell Place as well as in some suburbs. **Paddy Power** outlets can be found on MacCurtain Street, Shandon Street and Douglas Street. **Cashmans Bookmakers** are based at 1 Maylor Street (Tel: (021) 427 1770).

Cork sporting heroes

Christy Ring (1920-1979) – Hurler

The hurler from Cloyne in east county Cork is still widely regarded as one of the greatest hurlers to have ever graced the field. He played for Cork for 20 years and he won eight all-Ireland medals before he retired from the game in 1963. Testament to his continued popularity among the Cork people is the fact that a stadium and a bridge are named after him.

Sonia O'Sullivan – Athlete

Hailing from Cobh, Sonia O'Sullivan is one of the greatest athletes Ireland has ever produced. The long-distance runner won a silver medal in the 5000m at the 2000 Olympics. Throughout the 1990s she won several world grand prix and took world and European titles, breaking a couple of world records along the way.

Roy Keane – Soccer player

The Manchester United midfielder is from Mayfield in Cork city and began his career playing for Cobh Ramblers. As well as becoming one of Manchester Utd's most important players, Keane played for the Republic of Ireland in the World Cup finals in 1994, and went on to captain the team. He helped Ireland qualify for the 2002 World Cup Finals. However, Keane caused huge controversy when he was sent home before the finals even began following a row with manager Mick McCarthy. He subsequently retired from international football, much to the dismay of Irish fans, but made his return in 2004. He continues to play for Manchester Utd.

Part Two

SURROUNDING AREAS

8 OUTSKIRTS OF CORK CITY

Blarney

A small village situated 8 km north-west of Cork city, Blarney is one of the most popular tourist destinations in Ireland due to the famous castle that was built there in 1446 by Dermot MacCarthy who was King of Munster. The tourist office there is open year round (Tel: (021) 438 1624).

What is now known as **Blarney Castle** (Tel: (021) 438 5252) is in fact the keep of what was a much larger fortress. One of the main draws of the castle is the opportunity to kiss the famous **Blarney Stone** which is supposed to bestow the gift of eloquent speech, or the 'gift of the gab' on the kisser. The act of kissing the stone is not for the faint-hearted as it is placed high up in the tower, just below the parapets. To kiss it, it is necessary to lie on your back and lean your head backwards while holding on to iron bars. The castle is interesting to ramble around, but the notion that it is one of Ireland's most interesting tourist attractions is really a load of old blarney. County Cork has a lot more to offer than this. Open Mon–Sat, 9 a.m.–7 p.m. June–August, 9 a.m.–6.30 p.m. May & September, 9 a.m. to sundown October–April. On Sundays, the castle is open 9 a.m.–5.30 p.m. in summer or 9 a.m. to sundown in winter.

Next to the grounds of the castle is **Blarney Woollen Mills** which sells good quality handmade knitwear, Irish linen and Waterford Crystal alongside tacky souvenirs and leprechaun

Blarney Castle

hats to the bus loads of tourists visiting the castle. Open Mon–Sat, 9.30 a.m.–6 p.m., Sundays 10 a.m.–6 p.m.

In Cloghroe, a few kilometres outside Blarney, **Blair's Inn** (Tel: (021) 438 1470) is an award-winning pub on the river's edge that serves excellent food. The speciality is freshly cooked seafood. The restaurant is open from 6.30 in the evenings, but the bar menu is served all day. Trad sessions take place on Monday nights.

Phelan's Woodview House (Tel: (021) 438 5197), a little outside Blarney and adjacent to the Cork–Mallow Road, is also known for excellent food.

Farran Forest Park

Farran Forest Park is located about 18 km outside the city on the N22 to Macroom. The woods overlook the Lee reservoir in the hills of Iniscarra. There are lots of pleasant walks and good picnic spots; just watch out that the deer don't get to your lunch before you do. The wildlife reservoir has two species of deer and several types of waterfowl. There's a good adventure play area for kids and an ecology display housed in the restored hunting lodge. The National Rowing Centre is also located here and the Irish Amateur Rowing Championships usually take place on the lake in July. Admission to the park is €3 per car. Tel: (021) 733 6149.

Fota Wildlife Park and Fota House and Gardens

Just 10 km from the city, an easy drive or train ride away, Fota makes a great day trip for adults and kids. By car, take the N25 and turn off for the Cobh Road. There is a direct train from Cork to Fota, it takes about 15 minutes. The 70 acres holds a fantastic wildlife park that you can roam about freely, admiring over ninety species of wildlife, from tigers and cheetahs to zebras and giraffes. The monkeys and kangaroos are always a hit with kids. The animals roam about freely with the minimum amount of fencing. Feeding times are usually early morning and late afternoon.

The park was set up in 1983 as a joint venture between the Zoological Society of Ireland and UCC to breed endangered species. It is enjoyable to walk around but if you don't feel up to it, you can hop on the Wildlife Train. There are a couple of good play areas for children, and a number of picnic areas as well as a self-service restaurant.

Fota Wildlife Park

The park is open daily from 10 a.m.–5 p.m. on weekdays and from 11 a.m.–5 p.m. on Sundays. Admission is €9.50, children €6. It's another €2 for the car park. For more information, Tel: (021) 481 2678 or see *www.fotawildlife.ie*.

Next to the park is **Fota House and Gardens**. In the 1820s John Barry hired architects to turn what was a modest hunting lodge into the grand residence that became Fota House. Built in an elegant Regency style, the house has seventy rooms and sixty fireplaces, and is surrounded by magnificent grounds that include a 150-year-old arboretum. A large-scale restoration project began in 1999, and the house was officially opened to the public in 2002.

The Tea Room in the house serves light lunches and homemade cakes from 11 a.m. to 4 p.m. The house is open from 1 April to 30 September, Mon–Sat 10 a.m. to 5.30 p.m., and Sun 11 a.m. to 5.30 p.m. (last admissions at 4.30).

From 1 Oct to 30 March, the house is open Mon–Sat 11 a.m. to 4 p.m. with last admissions at 3.30. The admission price is €5 for adults, €2 for children. Tel: (021) 481 5543. See *www.fotahouse.com*.

Crosshaven and surrounding areas

West of Cork Harbour are plenty of small beaches and coves and seaside villages that are less than a half hour drive from the city. Getting to many of these places is difficult without a car, although buses do run from the bus station in Parnell Place to Crosshaven, Myrtleville and Fountainstown.

Not too long ago, Carrigaline was a small village but has now mushroomed into a satellite town with a growing commuter population of about 16,000. This growth has resulted in a sprawl of housing estates and increased traffic congestion. If you take a left at the roundabout in the centre of the Carrigaline, signposts will lead you to the small port village of **Crosshaven**. The village climbs the surrounding hills overlooking the sea. It is an important yachting centre and is home to the **Royal Cork Yacht Club** which was founded in 1720. There is a large marina and an active boat yard. There are some pleasant walks around the village. One such walk will lead you to the eighteenth-century **Fort Camden**, where the British army once had a base. **Cronin's Pub** by the bus stop in the centre of the village was originally built as the Railway Hotel (the railway closed in 1932). It serves excellent pub food and is a good place to look for local knowledge.

About 3 km beyond Crosshaven is the tiny seaside village of **Myrtleville**. The village leads down to a small beach which is safe for swimming but can be busy in summer and is not always clean. Just above the beach is **Bunnyconnellans Pub and**

Restaurant (Tel: (021) 483 1213) which has a pleasant garden with plenty of outdoor seating and good sea views. **Pine Lodge** in Myrtleville hosts regular live music gigs, and often serves bus loads of music fans from Cork city as well as locals. There is a clifftop walk from Myrtleville to the nearby **Fountainstown**, a long, pebbly stretch of beach. The walk is not too taxing and very scenic.

If you drive back towards Carrigaline as far as Minane Bridge and follow the signposts to **Robert's Cove** you'll find another seaside village that consists of two pubs, a mobile home park and a small, sandy beach. There is a picturesque clifftop walk just past the pubs. Near Robert's Cove is **Seán na mBád's Pub** (Tel: (021) 488 7397) which has an excellent reputation for good food and good pints in a convivial atmosphere. City dwellers regularly travel there for Sunday lunch or afternoon pints.

From Robert's Cove, follow signposts for **Nohoval** where you will find the **Finders Inn** (Tel: (021) 477 0737) which is known for its excellent food. About a mile from the village, Nohoval Cove is never too busy due to the sharp rocks and lack of sand, or perhaps due to the fact that it is so difficult to find. When the tide is out, it can be rather uninviting, but when the tide's in, it is a great spot for swimming or chilling out.

In Nohoval Village there are also signs for **Rocky Bay** which is actually more sandy than rocky and is a good beach for swimming and sandcastle building. When the weather's good, however, it can often be very busy and overrun by kids.

Oysterhaven is a sheltered cove a little further along the coast. It is popular for watersports due to the **Oysterhaven Activity Centre** which offers windsurfing and sailing courses. Although there is no village, as such, at Oysterhaven, there is a good restaurant, **Oz Haven** (Tel: (021) 477 0947), which is a more expensive relation of Oz Cork in the city.

Cobh

The maritime town of **Cobh** (pronounced Cove) is located just 12 km east of the city, so makes an easy day trip. It is built on the side of a steep hill that rises up from the sea. The twentieth-century Gothic cathedral dominates the townscape and is a well-known landmark.

To get there by car, take the N25 from Cork towards Midleton and turn off on the R624 following the signs for Cobh. Regular trains run from Cork to Cobh daily and the bus service is also regular but can take longer.

Cobh

There is no tourist office in Cobh but information can be obtained from the Cork Tourist Office on the Grand Parade in the city (Tel: (021) 425 5100).

Cobh is a relatively young town; its history dates back to the seventeenth century. It was called Queenstown from Queen Victoria's visit in 1849 until Irish independence was achieved in 1922. It has a long maritime history. The first steamship to cross the Atlantic, the *Sirius*, departed from Cobh in 1838. Following the Great Famine in the late 1840s, Cobh became the country's main emigration port. It is estimated that around two and half million people emigrated from there in the hundred years following the famine. The port was also the last port of call of the ill-fated *Titanic* in 1912.

Housed in the old Cobh railway station, the impressive **Queenstown Heritage Centre** (Tel: (021) 481 3591) has been established to commemorate those who were forced to depart from the port due to the potato famine. (See p. 33 for more information.)

The twentieth-century neo-Gothic **St Colman's Cathedral** stands 300 ft above sea level and dominates the town. The eponymous St Colman founded the diocese of Cloyne in AD 590. The cathedral was built over forty-seven years between 1868 and 1915, and there is a bell for each of those years in the carillion. The intricate carvings tell the story of the Church in Ireland from the time of St Patrick up until the present day.

A daily guided walking tour, known as the **Titanic Trail**, leaves daily at 11 a.m. from the Commodore Hotel in the town centre. The walk takes one and a half hours and covers the pier from which the *Titanic* passengers departed, the site of landing of the *Lusitania* victims and St Colman's Cathedral, with plenty of local history. The €7.50 charge includes a drink of Guinness in Jack Doyle's Bar. The tour finishes up in the Titanic Queenstown Bar & Grill. The same people also organize a

Ghost Walk which claims to visit Cobh's most haunted sites. For more information, Tel: (021) 481 5211 or log on to *www.titanic-trail.com*.

The **Sirius Arts Centre** is a non-profit centre opened in 1988 to fill the gap in arts facilities in East Cork and is well worth a visit. Housed in the renovated Old Yacht Club, the centre regularly holds art exhibitions as well as showcasing local musical and literary talent and organizing workshops. Open Wed–Fri 11 a.m.–5 p.m., Sat & Sun 2 p.m.–5 p.m. (Tel: (021) 481 3790).

The newly refurbished **Rushbrooke Hotel** (Tel: (021) 481 2242) sits on the water's edge and offers ensuite bedrooms from €45 upwards. The facilities include a waterfront bar and restaurant and a massage clinic and beauty spa. See *www.rushbrookehotel.ie*. The **Water's Edge Hotel** (Tel: (021) 481 5566) is on the waterfront next to the Cobh Heritage Centre. Tastefully decorated rooms go from €50 per person sharing.

Jacob's Ladder Restaurant (Tel: (021) 481 5566) in the Water's Edge hotel has an excellent reputation. It serves 'Irish continental cuisine with a twist'. The **Titanic Queenstown Bar and Restaurant** (Tel: (021) 485 5200) has to be seen to be believed. Built by a lottery winner in the old White Star buildings, the restaurant replicates the Verdanah Room aboard the ill-fated liner, while the main bar is styled on the second-class smoking room. Food prices are reasonable.

Kinsale

The picturesque harbour village of Kinsale is about 18 miles from Cork and is a popular destination for day trips or weekend visits. The village has a long U-shaped waterfront, with narrow winding streets filled with gourmet restaurants

Kinsale

and craft shops, making it a lovely place to wander around. Compass Hill rises up behind the town offering some magnificent sea views.

Sea angling, Kinsale

It is a popular centre for sailing and deep-sea fishing. It has also built up a reputation as a culinary centre and has some excellent restaurants. Kinsale gets very busy during the summer months, especially July and August. The place can be extremely quiet, on the other hand, in January and February, with many restaurants closing for those months.

During the May bank holiday weekend (first weekend in May), the **Kinsale Rugby Sevens** takes place, which is often as much about drinking and socializing as it is about rugby. The **Kinsale Regatta** takes place during the August bank holiday weekend (first weekend in August) and a **Gourmet Food Festival** takes place in early October.

The **Kinsale Tourist Office** (Tel: (021) 477 2234) is located right in the centre of the town next to the bus office on Pier Road. The office is open from 9.30 a.m. to 5.30 p.m.

History

Some of the earliest settlers in Ireland are believed to have based themselves at the Old Head of Kinsale. The town received its first royal charter in 1333, and its history was pretty uneventful until 1601 when the famous **Battle of Kinsale** took place. A Spanish fleet arrived at Kinsale Harbour at the request of Irish Chieftains, Red Hugh O'Donnell and Hugh O'Neill, to join forces with the Irish to fight Queen Elizabeth's forces. However, the plan backfired and they were defeated. Kinsale was back in English hands by 2 January, 1602.

In 1689, **James II** landed in Kinsale after the English Parliament had objected to his ascension to the throne and replaced him with the Protestant William of Orange. The Siege of Cork and the decisive Battle of the Boyne took place in 1690 and James was defeated.

Narrow street, Kinsale

Kinsale entered the history books again in 1915 when the American liner, the *Lusitania*, was sank 14 miles off the Old Head of Kinsale. It had been attacked by a German submarine and nearly 1,200 people were killed. The event led to the US entering World War I. Three of the victims of the *Lusitania* are buried in the churchyard of **St Multose Church**.

Places to visit

The inquest into the tragedy took place in Kinsale and the courtroom is preserved and has been turned into the **Kinsale Museum** (Tel: (021) 477 7930). The courthouse building was built in 1600, while the Dutch-style façade dates back to the early 1700s. The museum also houses memorabilia from the *Lusitania*. It is open Wed 10.30 a.m.–3 p.m., Thurs–Sun 10.30 a.m.–4.15 p.m., closed Monday and Tuesday. Admission is €2.50. **Desmond Castle** on Cork Street, also in the town centre, is a restored sixteenth-century tower. Guided tours are available.

Charles Fort is a National Monument located about two miles outside the town near an area called Summercove. The star-shaped fort was built as a coastal defence in 1677 and spans nine acres. It has been restored and most of the ramparts and bastions are still intact. Charles Fort was garrisoned until 1922. It is now open from April to October and guided tours are usually available.

By crossing the bridge that spans the Bandon River just outside the town and then turning left, you can reach **James Fort** which was built in the early 1600s. It is not restored but the ruins have their own charm and are fun to ramble around. In front of the fort is the **Dock Bar**, which is a pleasant place to sit outside and have a drink on a sunny day. About 200 yards away is a sandy beach that is a good spot for swimming or windsurfing.

Places to stay

The three star **Acton's Hotel** (Tel: (021) 477 2135) overlooking the harbour is right at the heart of Kinsale. It is surrounded by pleasant gardens and has a well-equipped health and fitness club. There is an excellent restaurant, **The Captain's Table**, and a bar, The Waterfront, which also serves good food. Rooms go from €70 to €150 per person sharing. See *www.actonshotelkinsale.com*. The **Trident Hotel** (Tel: (021) 477 2301) also has three stars and also overlooks the water. There is a leisure centre and a private marina for yachts. Room rates range from €55 to €150 per person sharing. The **Savannah Restaurant** is a member of the Good Food Circle.

The Old Presbytery on Cork Street (Tel: (021) 477 2027) is a 200-year-old Georgian townhouse that provides bed & (a very good) breakfast and self-catering accommodation from €35 to €75 per person sharing. More exclusive is **The Old Bank House** at 11 Pearse Street (Tel: (021) 477 2075). The old Georgian residence's claim to fame is that it has been voted one of the 'Top 100 Places to Stay in Ireland' by the Bridgestone Guide every year since 1990. It is easy to see why, with luxurious rooms and great character, but expect to pay for it with room rates from €175 to €260 per room. At the other end of the price scale, the newly renovated **Guardwell Lodge Hostel** (Tel: (021) 477 4684) offers excellent value for money with beds from €15 to €25 depending on the size of the room. It is right in the centre of town and has good kitchen facilities. See *www.kinsalehostel.com*.

Places to eat

Kinsale is known as a culinary centre and is home to many fine restaurants. Please note that many of the restaurants close for at least some of the winter season, which can be any time between October and March.

Possibly the best-known is **Man Friday** in Scilly (Tel: (021) 477 2260) which has been run by the chef Philip Horgan for eighteen years. It's open Mon–Sat from 7 p.m. to 10.30 p.m. It is expensive but worth splashing out for. **Crackpots Restaurant** at 3 Cork Street (Tel: (021) 477 2847) serves local seafood on homemade pottery that is also for sale and is open from 6 p.m.–10 p.m. **The Vintage Restaurant** at 50 Main Street (Tel: (021) 477 2502) is known for excellent, very expensive Irish and continental cuisine. It's open from 6.30 p.m. (closed from January to mid-February). **Max's Wine Bar** at 48 Main Street (Tel: (021) 477 2260) serves Irish and French cuisine and is one of the best spots in town for Sunday lunch, although it is open every day except Tuesday for lunch and dinner.

Eating out in Kinsale can be expensive so if you're on a budget, it might be wiser to stop for lunch. **Fishy Fishy Café**

Kinsale

(Tel: (021) 477 4453) serves fresh seafood in relaxed surroundings from 12 noon to 3.45 p.m. daily. The **Lord Kingsale** on Main Street (Tel: (021) 477 2731) is also a good spot for lunch; their homemade soups are famous. Lunch is served Mon–Fri 12–4.

The Bulman Bar & Restaurant in Summercove (Tel: (021) 477 2131) is on the water's edge and has good views. The restaurant serves Mediterranean and Asian-influenced food and is open from 12.30 p.m. to 9.30 p.m. The bar can be quite lively, especially on summer evenings. **The Spaniard** in Scilly (Tel: (021) 477 2436) is known as one of Kinsale's liveliest bars. It also has a restaurant open from 6.30 p.m. and serves good pub grub during the day. Closer to the town centre, the **Greyhound Bar** by Market Square is cosy and has a good atmosphere.

9 WEST CORK

There are a number of routes west. By going through Bandon to Clonakilty and then on to Skibbereen, there is ample opportunity to visit sweeping, sandy beaches and rocky coves as well as picturesque coastal villages. From Skibbereen, one road will bring you towards the fishing village of Baltimore, from which you can reach Sherkin Island or the wilder Cape Clear. Another road will take you through Ballydehob to the sheltered harbour where you will find the popular village of Schull. From Schull, you can continue on through Goleen along a road that offers some of the most dramatic scenery in West Cork to the tiny village of Crookhaven and the nearby sand dunes and beach of Barleycove. It is not too far from here to Mizen Head, the most southerly point of Ireland, and certainly one of the most spectacular.

Another route west will lead you through Bandon and Dunmanway to the sea town of Bantry and then on to Glengarriff's nature reserve. From here you can continue west to the untamed Castletownbere and nearby Bere Island, the real edge of Ireland.

Clonakilty

The residents of the market town of Clonakilty deserve full marks for effort when it comes to the upkeep of their town.

Many businesses have traditional shopfronts with handpainted signs in the Irish language, and brightly painted houses with blooming window boxes are the order of the day. A disused Gothic Presbyterian church is now the post office, while the library and town council offices are housed in a nineteenth-century mill. The town has won a National Tidy Towns Title four times since 1996. It is also Ireland's first and only Fair Trade Town, an initiative started up by a group of locals to encourage and promote the use of fair trade products in Clonakilty.

A farmers' market takes place on Thursdays.

There are eight buses a day from Cork with the journey taking 1hr 10m (note the Skibbereen bus stops here). The Tourist Office is located on Ashe Street (Tel: (023) 33226).

The town was founded by Richard Boyle, Great Earl of Cork, in 1605 and is best known as the birthplace of Michael Collins, a well-known hero of the War of Independence. The revolutionary leader fought in the 1916 Rising. In 1921 he was sent to London to negotiate the Anglo-Irish Treaty. Deciding it was the best possible deal available, he signed the Treaty, calling it a 'stepping stone' to the Republic. As Commander-in-Chief of the Free State Government, he was ambushed and killed on a military visit to Cork in 1922.

The **West Cork Museum** has many mementos of Michael Collins as well as items from the town's linen-making history. The **West Cork Model Railway Village** on Inchydoney Road (Tel: (023) 33224) has an impressive miniature representation of West Cork towns during the 1930s to 1950s and a fully automated model of the West Cork Railway that operated during this period. It is open daily from April to October, and at weekends throughout the rest of the year.

During the summer months, **Ardigeen Heritage Park** run

by Timothy and Dorothy Crowley offers 'Michael Collins' tours that take in his birthplace and the site of the ambush at Beal na Blath. The Crowleys also conduct guided walking tours around the Clonkilty area. To find out more, contact them on (023) 46107 or check out *www.reachireland.com*.

Lios na gCon (Lisnagun) Ring Fort just outside Clonakilty is the only ring fort in Ireland to be fully reconstructed on its original site. To get there, turn left at the roundabout that you meet coming into the town from Cork. Continue along that road until you reach the minuscule village of Ring and take a right turn here.

A couple of miles outside town on the other side is **Inchydoney Beach**, a long, wide, sandy beach sheltered by tall cliffs. It is a popular spot for swimming and for picnics. It is a short drive, but also a pleasant cycle from Clonakilty.

Places to stay

What the **Quality Hotel** on the western edge of the town (Tel: (023) 35400) lacks in character, it makes up for in facilities. It has ensuite rooms, two-room suites and a few self-catering houses, as well as a restaurant, a bar, a good leisure centre and a three-screen cinema complex. Room-only rates go from €69 to €199. If you'd rather stay in the centre of town, **Randles Clonakilty Hotel** on Wolfe Tone Street (Tel: (023) 34749) is an elegant three-star hotel. **The Town House** on Strand Road (Tel: (023) 35533) is a centrally-located guest house with big, comfortable rooms from €40 per person sharing.

Just outside the town, **Desert House** (Tel: (023) 33331) offers accommodation in a Georgian farmhouse near the water and overlooking the town. It also has a campsite for those brave enough. Turn left at the roundabout as you enter Clonakilty from Cork.

The **Old Brewery Hostel** (Tel: (023) 33525) on Old Brewery Lane just off Emmett Square offers dorm accommodation and private rooms.

The luxurious **Inchydoney Lodge and Spa** (Tel: (023) 33143) overlooks the beach. A room will set you back from €135 per person per night, while a weekend deal including two nights bed and breakfast and one dinner costs €295 per person. However, you don't have to be a resident to take advantage of the thalassotherapy spa. See *www.inchydoneyisland.com*.

Places to eat and drink

Clonakilty is well served for restaurants and lively bars. **An Súgán** at 41 Wolfe Tone Street (Tel: (023) 33498) is an award-winning pub and restaurant that's known for its good grub. On the same street, **Richy's Bar and Bistro** (Tel: (023) 21852) is a funky little restaurant with a reasonably priced and varied menu that includes salads, pastas, fajitas and Asian dishes.

Gleeson's is very expensive but the food is excellent if you're willing to splash out. **Gearóidín's** at 18 Pearse Street (Tel: (023) 34444) is a café by day and a restaurant serving steaks and seafood at night. If you're looking for some Eastern food, try the **Shama** restaurant on Ashe Street (Tel: (023) 36945) for authentic Indian dishes.

A trip to Clonakilty certainly wouldn't be complete without sampling the famous Clonakility black pudding. It is widely available from all butcher shops or supermarkets.

De Barras Folk Club at 55 Pearse Street (Tel: (023) 33381) is a live music pub that has an excellent sound system and hosts trad sessions and gigs most nights of the week. Many well-known bands who visit Cork city will often play at De Barras as well. Noel Redding, who was a member of the Jimi

Hendrix band, used to play here regularly until he passed away in 2003. **An Teach Beag** around the side of O'Donovans Hotel on Pearse Street is also a great place to go and hear some trad sessions; it tends to be very popular in the summertime. **Scannell's** is always packed, no matter what night of the week. **Con & Maura's Bar** on MacCurtain Hill is a small, quaint pub that's full of character (and characters).

Seven Heads Peninsula

South-east of Clonakilty, a maze of narrow roads connects the villages and beaches of what is known as the Seven Heads Peninsula. Many of these roads are poorly signposted and it is easy to get lost.

Timoleague is a well-kept village at the head of a sea inlet. It is a good starting point for exploring the peninsula. There is a well-preserved Franciscan abbey on the water's edge that dates back to the thirteenth century.

From Timoleague, follow signposts to **Courtmacsherry**, which is a popular holiday village with a small pier and surrounded by sandy beaches. Deep sea fishing, windsurfing and sailing are all on offer.

When the tide is out, **Dunworley Bay** reveals a sheltered, smooth, sandy beach that is not usually as busy as Inchydoney or Courtmacsherry (possibly because it is so difficult to find). Probably the easiest way to find it is to go through Timoleague, from where there are a few signposts. **Otto's Creative Cooking** at Dunworley (Tel: (023) 40461) is an excellent restaurant and cookery school that is part of the Slow Food Movement that promotes the use of fresh, seasonal, organic produce. Dinner costs €45 per head (Wed–Sun), while on Saturdays and Sundays, lunch is available for €30.

Clonakilty to Skibbereen

On the road from Clonakilty to Skibbereen, there are plenty more coastal villages to visit. Some of these are reached by side roads that run south to the sea from the main road.

The first such village is **Owenahincha**, a rundown, dated-looking seaside resort with holiday houses scattered all about. There is a stony beach in front of the main stretch of village, but there is a much more impressive sandy beach at **Castlefreke** just a little further down the road. Castlefreke Forest offers 7 km of walking trails, with picnic areas and a car park, and right in the middle of the woods are the impressive ruins of the ancient Rathbarry castle. The castle was built in the fifteenth century by the Barry family and in the seventeenth century was acquired by the Frekes who gave it their name.

Further along the main Clonakilty-Skibbereen road, you will come to the small cathedral town of **Rosscarbery**. The Skibbereen bus stops at Rosscarbery; the bus trip from Cork takes about 1 hour, 25 mins. A causeway bridges a deep inlet from Rosscarbery Bay so that, as you drive into the village, you will see a sea marsh to your left and a swan-inhabited lake to your right. Rosscarbery grew up around a monastery founded by St Fachtna in the sixth century, although the area has been occupied since long before then as the Neolithic Portal Dolmens show. If you take a right turn as you enter the town, you will arrive at the town square, which was once its market place. **St Fachtna's Cathedral** is a short walk from the square. An **Arts & Literature Festival** takes place in May. For information, go to *www.rosscarbery.ie*.

You can't miss the three-star **Celtic Ross Hotel** (Tel: (023) 48722) as you arrive into Rosscarbery. Unfortunately, it has taken somewhat from the aesthetic of the town. It has a bar, restaurant and leisure centre. Rates start at €70 per night. For fresh, organic food, try **Pilgrim's Rest** at 6 South Square (Tel: (023) 48063).

A little outside the town, in the direction of Glandore, is **Drombeg Stone Circle**, known locally as the Druids Altar, dating to the Bronze Age. At the Winter Solstice (21 December), the sun sets into a hollow between two hills in the west in alignment with the stones of the circle and the rays of the setting sun fall on the flat altar stone. Archaeological excavations have revealed a nearby 'fulacht fiadh' which was a cooking area that involved throwing hot stones from a fire into a pit of water to heat it.

Blink and you'll miss the tiny village of **Leap** back on the main road to Skibbereen. It is worth keeping your eyes open for the near-legendary **Connolly's of Leap** (Tel: (028) 33215) on the right-hand side of the road, however. It's one of the best live music venues in the county, if not the country. It is not uncommon for touring bands visiting the main cities to include Leap on their itinerary. It is also a friendly place to stop for a pint on your way west. For gig listings, check out *www.connollysofleap.com*.

The Irish name for Leap is Léim Uí Dhonnabháin, meaning O'Donovan's Leap. It comes from an old legend about a local chieftain, O'Donovan, who escaped British soldiers by jumping across the ravine at the western edge of the village. Before the road bridged the ravine, there were no law enforcers west of it, giving rise to the saying 'beyond the Leap, beyond the law'.

By taking a detour off to the left from Leap, you will reach the quiet haven of **Glandore**, a pretty village rising up a hill overlooking a land-locked harbour. Its population expands dramatically in the summertime as the many summer houses around the area fill up for the season. **Hayes Bar** has outside seating that overlooks the water and the seafood is excellent.

Across the water is another picturesque fishing village,

Union Hall. Maria's Schoolhouse (Tel: (028) 33002) was the Union Hall National School for over one hundred years. It has been beautifully renovated and converted into a hostel and activity centre. Dorm beds are available from €15, while a family room that sleeps four costs €64. There is a cosy hangout area and colourful dining room, and the building has real character. See *www.mariasschoolhouse.com*. Dinty's Bar serves wonderful pub grub, although at restaurant prices.

The Union Hall Festival held every June is based around watersports of both serious and just-for-fun varieties.

Sea angling and kayaking are popular activities around Union Hall and Glandore due to the clean waters of the harbour. Those brave enough to venture sea kayaking trips along the coast should contact **Atlantic Sea Kayaking** (Tel: (028) 21058), run by Jim Kennedy. They organize half day, full day and moonlight kayak trips as well as longer tours for the more adventurous. See *www.atlanticseakayaking.com*. **Glandore & Union Hall Sea Angling** organizes angling trips around the harbour and in nearby lakes. Contact Geraldine O'Neill in Leap on (028) 33510.

Back on the main Skibbereen road, there is another turn off a few kilometres further on for unspoiled **Castletownshend**. The main street runs down to the edge of Castlehaven Harbour and is lined with large eighteenth-century stone houses. The junction marked by two sycamore trees is crossed by the Mall. Yachts line the small marina, and a regatta takes place every July.

It is worth climbing the steps to **St Barrahane's church**, perched on a hill with a magnificent view of the harbour. You can admire the Harry Clarke stained glass window behind the altar or simply admire the view. During July and August, a classical music festival takes place there. Castletownshend was the home of the famous writer and artist Edith Somerville, who died in 1949. She is buried at St Barrahane's. The church overlooks the castle, which is now used as a guesthouse called,

Castletownshend

aptly, *The Castle* (Tel: (028) 36100). **Mary Ann's Bar & Restaurant** is famous for good seafood. You can order pub grub from the bar or splash out on a more formal meal in the restaurant area. It's a good spot for a few creamy pints of stout in the evenings as well.

Skibbereen

Skibbereen is the last major town you'll come across as you venture further into West Cork so is a good place to stock up in supplies. It is a busy market town on the River Ilen dating back to 1631.

Before the Great Famine, Skibbereen was an important

centre for woollen and linen cloth manufacturing. The town was badly hit by the potato famine in the mid-1840s. It is believed that there are up to 10,000 famine victims buried at Abbetstrewery Cemetery. It played an important role in the War of Independence in the early twentieth century and the town's trade and industry suffered badly from the ensuing civil war.

The tourist office (Tel: (028) 21766) located in the Town Hall on North Street distributes Skibbereen Trail maps. Buses stop outside O'Cahalanes on Bridge Street where you can get timetable information. There are several buses daily from Cork and the journey takes 1 hour 50 mins.

Skibbereen Heritage Centre (Tel: (028) 40900) organizes historical walking tours covering from pre-Christian times to present day. The walks leave from the heritage centre at 6.30 p.m. on Tuesdays and Saturdays. The centre, which is housed in an old gasworks building, also has a Great Famine Commemoration Exhibition and a Lough Hyne Visitor Centre that explains this unique saltwater lake.

The **West Cork Arts Centre** in the Sutherland Centre on North Street (Tel: (028) 22090) exhibits work from artists based in the West Cork area as well as hosting exhibitions from further afield. It is open Monday–Friday, 10 a.m.–5 p.m.

Places to stay

There are two hotels in Skibbereen but there are plenty of B&Bs in the area. Contact the tourist office or look up *www.corkkerry.ie* for a comprehensive list.

The **West Cork Hotel** on Ilen Street (Tel: (028) 21277) is the bigger and better-known of the town's two hotels. The traditional hotel has been sitting right on the river for over a century. Rooms are available from €50 per person in low season and from €80 per person in high season. **The Eldon Hotel** on

Bridge Street (Tel: (028) 22000) is where Michael Collins had his last meal and made his last speech before he was assassinated in 1922. Rates are €44 in low season and €80 in high season.

Russagh Mill Hostel and Adventure Centre (Tel: (028) 22451) is located in a beautiful stone building that was once a corn mill. The centre offers dorm accommodation from €12 per person and private rooms from €15. Kayaking and climbing trips are available. Open from mid-April to the end of October.

About a kilometre outside Skibbereen in the direction of Castletownshend are the beautifully landscaped gardens of the **Liss Ard Foundation** (Tel: (028) 22365). The conservation project spans 50 acres and includes a woodland garden, a wildflower meadow, a lakeside walk and a waterfall garden. Most interesting is the Irish Sky Garden designed by artist James Turrell. Full garden tours are available on Tuesday and Thursday at 4.30 p.m. The tours last about one and a half hours and booking is necessary. Open from May to September.

About 5 km outside Skibbereen towards Baltimore are **Creagh Gardens** (Tel: (028) 22121) which consist of 20 acres of woodlands with a network of paths and trails that slope down towards the water's edge. The gardens are open daily all year. There is a small admission fee.

Lough Hyne, about 5 km south of Skibbereen, is Europe's largest saltwater lake and Ireland's first Marine Nature Reserve. The lake is fed from the sea by a narrow tidal channel and is home to many unusual marine species, ensuring a constant stream of marine biologists to the area. It is surrounded by trees and hills and is a beautiful spot for walking or picnicking, as well as for swimming.

From Skibbereen, there are a number of routes you can take into the depths of west Cork. The main road west will lead you to Ballydehob, from where you can turn off for Durrus and Bantry or continue straight on to Schull and the Mizen Peninsula.

Baltimore, Sherkin and Cape Clear

About 12 km south of Skibereen is the fishing village of **Baltimore**, although yachting seems to be a more prominent activity than fishing these days. To get there by bus, you must take the expressway bus to Skibbereen and then take a local bus (no. 215). This bus only runs from Monday to Friday (Saturdays in summer) and is not too regular, so be sure to check out the timetable before planning your trip.

The harbour looks out on and is protected by an archipelago known as Carbery's Hundred Isles, which includes the inhabited islands of Sherkin and Cape Clear. The village itself revolves around the pier, and is quite lively during the summer months as visitors arrive to take the ferry to the islands or just to spend a day admiring the views from the mainland. Although the area has been almost overrun with holiday houses, the village itself still retains its charm. The ruins of a sixteenth-century O'Driscoll castle overlook the harbour. The O'Driscolls were the most powerful clan in the area for many centuries, and each June, an O'Driscoll family gathering lasting five days takes place all over Baltimore, Sherkin and Cape Clear.

The O'Driscoll clan had a long-running feud with the fishing port of Waterford that began as early as the fourteenth century. In 1631, Algerian pirates were led into Baltimore by a Waterford man and two of his ships. The pirates kidnapped about 200 inhabitants (most of the population) and shipped them off as slaves to Algeria.

The village now has a population of about 200, but this number grows greatly in the summertime. As well as attracting daytrippers and holidaymakers, summer sailing courses attract plenty of teenagers from the city. The sailing regatta takes place around the end of July and beginning of August and always attracts a large crowd. The place is also popular with fans of

Loch Hyne, near Baltimore

windsurfing, waterskiing and deep sea diving. For waterskiing, contact **Atlantic Boating Service** on (028) 22734 or on *www.atlanticboat.ie*. For diving trips, try **Aquaventures** on (028) 20511. See *www.aquaventures.ie*.

There are great views of the islands to be had if you walk up the hill behind the village towards the white beacon.

The three-star **Baltimore Bay Hotel** (Tel: (028) 20361) overlooking the harbour has comfortable, modern rooms from €60 per person. It also has a few luxury suites, as well as a bar, restaurant and leisure centre. **Casey's Hotel** (Tel: (028) 20197) also overlooks the harbour. The family-run hotel is smaller and has a little more character. Bed and breakfast goes from €64 in low season and from €77 in high season. The pub there serves good bar food and there is also a good seafood restaurant with views of the sea.

Rolf's Holiday Hostel (Tel: (028) 20289) is built in a renovated old stone farmhouse with a pretty garden and courtyard area. Dorm accommodation is available from €13 and double/twin rooms cost €40. There are also some two-bedroomed cottages that sleep four. As well as offering good value accommodation, there's also a good quality, good value restaurant, **Café Art**.

There are a few pubs looking out on the harbour; most have outside seating in summertime and the place tends to become quite lively at night during the summer months.

Sherkin Island is a ten-minute ferry trip from Baltimore and provides a beautiful and peaceful sanctuary from the real world. The island, which is 5 km long and one and a half wide, has leafy, narrow roadways with barely any motorized traffic, and on its west side are white sandy beaches. There is an independent marine research centre on the island. There are the remains of a fifteenth-century friary and another ruined O'Driscoll castle, Dún na Long. The island's two pubs, **The**

Jolly Roger and **The Islander's Rest**, are across the road from one another. Both serve pub grub, and the latter also provides en-suite accommodation. From June to October, ferries go from Baltimore hourly from 9.30 a.m. to 8.30 p.m. Outside these months, there are usually three ferries a day. For timetable information, Tel: (028) 20218.

The ferry to the island of **Cape Clear** (Oileán na Chléire) takes about an hour. The island, which is about the same size as Sherkin, is a Gaeltacht, meaning that Irish is spoken by the inhabitants, and during the summer months, flocks of secondary school students come to stay on the island to practise their Irish. The landscape of Cape Clear is more rugged than that of nearby Sherkin, with steep cliffs and gorse-covered hills. The island is almost divided in two at North Harbour and South Harbour, with two sea inlets almost meeting. The north harbour is the more sheltered and thus the busier of the two, and this is where the ferry will drop you off. The village, **Cummer**, straddles the land between the north and south harbours. The islanders, known as Capers, are notorious for their clannishness. They see themselves as a people apart and refer to the mainland as Ireland.

During the American Civil War, the south harbour was used as a communication centre with a submarine telegraph cable that was linked to Baltimore, Dublin and Europe. American ships would drop off mails into the sea in waterproof wrapping and the messages would then be communicated to the rest of Europe via telegraph.

Cape Clear's history goes back much further than the American Civil War though. It is believed to be the birthplace of St Ciaran, who was born in the fourth century. Many maintain that he brought Christianity to Ireland before St Patrick did, and there is a pilgrimage on 5 March each year, his feast day. Near the harbour, you can see the remains of the

Cape Clear Island

twelfth-century St Ciaran's church, built on the site of his original settlement. If you make the effort to walk to the top of the steep hill that rises out of the harbour, you will be able to look across at yet another O'Driscoll castle, Dun an Oir, which stands on a narrow rock that was once accessible by a causeway but is now almost impossible to get to. Also, over the hill is Lough Errol, the water of which has special cleansing properties due to rare micro-organisms.

There is no tourist office as such on the island but the pottery shop on the pier also serves as an information centre. The village has a shop and three pubs. There is a basic hostel at South Harbour (Tel: (028) 39198), about 10 minutes' walk from the pier, and sea kayaking and diving trips can be booked from here. At the top of the steep hill behind North Harbour is the island's heritage centre. Bird watchers will be delighted by the ornithological centre; Cape Clear has some rare species of seabirds. Accommodation is also available at the centre (Tel: (028) 39181).

Cape Clear Island

Every September, the **Story-telling Festival** attracts visitors from all over the globe to the island. For information on the year's programme, look up *www.oilean-chleire.ie*. Much of the action takes place in the island's three pubs, Cotter's, Ciaran Danny Mike's and The Club, all within five minutes of each other.

Ferries to and from Baltimore leave four times a day during summer, and less often during winter (Tel: (028) 39135). Between November and February, weather may prevent the ferry from sailing. Boats leave for Cape Clear from Schull as well in July and August (Tel: (028) 28138).

Skibbereen to Ballydehob

Back on the main road from Skibbereen to Ballydehob, it is well worth taking time out to visit **The Island Cottage** on **Hare Island** (Tel: (028) 38102) for a unique eating experience. It is necessary to book well in advance (months ahead sometimes) and it is only open from May to September. To get there, turn left off the main road at Church Cross and follow the signposts for Cunnamore until the road ends at Cunnamore Pier car park. You will be taken in a ferry across to the island and after arriving at the restaurant, will be told what you will be eating for your multi-course meal and you can choose from the wine menu. The set menu is €35 per person and is well worth the expense if you can afford it. Cookery courses are also available.

Ballydehob is a colourful little village at the top of a sea inlet with a twelve-arched railway bridge. It is a quiet spot but has some good pubs and restaurants. European exiles and artists live side by side with local farmers. Some of the buses from Cork go as far as Ballydehob, but they are few and far between, as most only go as far as Clonakilty or Skibbereen.

The best chocolate cake in the world exists in **Annie's Restaurant** on Main Street (Tel: (028) 37292), a great spot for top-quality simple food cooked at an affordable price, along with a bit of craic from Annie herself. It seats only a few and has set dinner times and menus so you will need to book ahead in summer. Across the road is **Levis** which is a grocery store and a pub in one. It is run by two elderly sisters who are famous characters and is one of the few remaining half shop/half pubs in the country. You can order food from Annie's while enjoying a pint in Levis and they will call you when it's ready.

Schull

Schull is a prosperous fishing village overlooked by Mount Gabriel which makes a good base for exploring the Mizen Peninsula. There are only a couple of buses a day that go from Cork all the way to Schull. The journey takes about 2 hours.

The population swells at weekends and especially during the summer as city dwellers make their escape to the west. On the main street, gourmet food shops, cafés and craft shops sit comfortably alongside old pubs and chip shops. It is a popular spot for sailing and watersports, and the sailing courses in July mean that the town is overrun with teenagers. There is a sailing regatta at the beginning of August. The **Watersports Centre** on the pier organizes sailing, windsurfing and sea angling trips. If all the watersports get too much, you can take a break to look at the stars instead in Ireland's only planetarium, located in Scoil Mhuire, the secondary school on Colla Road. The farmers' market on a Saturday morning is always lively. Nowadays, you will hear more French and Spanish accents than Irish from behind the stalls. There are plenty of good walks around here as well, including the trek up to the top of Mount Gabriel, from where there are stunning views of land and sea. A ferry runs every day in summer from Schull to Cape Clear island.

Fastnet Lighthouse

The Backpackers Lodge on Colla Road (Tel: (028) 28691) is an excellent hostel not far from the main streets. The wooden building is clean, well-run and comfortable. There are plenty of B&Bs and guest houses, but many visitors to Schull prefer to take the self-catering option as there are plenty of good holiday home developments around the town. **Colla House Hotel** (Tel: (028) 28105), about 3 km out the same road, has an unspoilt view of the sea and really gives the feel of being away from it all. Rooms cost €35–€55 per person sharing.

On Main Street, the **Courtyard** (Tel: (028) 28390) is a cosy pub with a gourmet food shop and café at the front, and a decent Thai restaurant in the evenings. There is usually live music in the pub part at night, and on warmer evenings, you can drink outside in the courtyard area. Even if you don't stop to eat there, pick up some of their delicious brown bread, known locally as 'the lump'. **La Coquille** is a Bridgestone-recommended restaurant run by a French chef, well known for its seafood. **Adele's** (Tel: (028) 28459) across the road can be a little pricey for a coffee shop but does serve very good food. **The Bunratty Inn** (Tel: (028) 28341) at the top of Main Street, across the road from the library, serves excellent pub grub and good stout too. You can defrost next to the roaring fireplace in winter or hang out in the beer garden at the back in summertime. It's not a bad spot for bringing kids to either. **The Waterside Bar** serves decent enough pub grub, while **Hackett's Pub** tends to draw a more alternative crowd. Both have regular live music sessions.

Schull to Mizen Head

If you continue west from Schull along the winding bog road, you will pass through the tiny village of **Toormore** and before arriving at the almost as tiny village of **Goleen**. The village was built in the nineteenth century at a crossroads where a cattle fair was held and most of the houses were originally built as shops. If you turn off at the signpost for Heron's Cove, you will come to a little harbour that dries out at high tide. The fantastic **Heron's Cove Restaurant** (Tel: (028) 35225) is open only in the summer months. As well as a top-quality restaurant, it is a small B&B with loads of character.

Goleen is the last stop on the Bus Eireann route, and there are only one or two buses that go this far, but if you can find a way to continue on towards **Mizen**, you will be well rewarded with some of the most spectacular scenery Ireland has to offer. On the way to Mizen, take a turn off to stop at Crookhaven which was for centuries the last port of call for ships on their way to America. Things are a bit quieter these days. Overlooking a sheltered harbour, **Crookhaven** is built on a small peninsula and consists of a pier and a handful of pubs, shops and guest houses. It has a population of less than 100, although that number swells greatly at weekends and in the summer. In fact, those looking for a quiet retreat might not find it here in summertime as throngs of city dwellers, many of them young, descend on the village. Have a pint or a toasted sandwich by the fire in O'Sullivans and look out over the water through the large front windows.

A couple of kilometres from here is **Barley Cove**, a long, wide, sandy beach with sand dunes behind it. There is a car park at the other side of the sand dunes. Barley Cove is probably one of the best beaches in the south-west and is a popular spot for surfing and swimming.

If you continue for about 5 km past Barley Cove, you'll finally reach **Mizen Head**, Ireland's most southerly point, and it will be well worth the trip. A lighthouse is placed on top of a rugged, rocky headland and to get to it, one must walk across a very high, narrow suspension bridge that links Mizen to the mainland. The lighthouse is now automated, but the surrounding buildings have

Mizen Head

been turned into a small museum that focuses on the lives of the lighthouse keepers. Mizen is stunning any day of the year but is at its most spectacular on a wild, windy day when the white foam of the sea lashes against the cliffs.

Durrus and Sheep's Head Peninsula

You can get to **Durrus** by going back through Goleen and turning off at Toormoor. If you don't want to go as far as Mizen Head, you can take a right turn at Ballydehob as you are driving west. This tiny village surrounded by hills is at the head of Dunmanus Bay but is set a little in from the sea.

Blairs Cove Restaurant (Tel: (027) 61127), facing on to the courtyard of the 250-year-old Georgian Blairs Cove House, is renowned for its excellent, if pricey, food and its atmospheric setting. It is open from March to October, and dinner is served between 7.30 p.m. and 9.30 p.m. Table d'hôte costs €50. Accommodation is also available from €85 per person sharing.

The recently opened **Good Things Café** (Tel: (027) 61426) specializes in homemade food using fresh, local produce. It is part of the growing slow food movement that is taking off in Cork. It is open four days a week – Thursday to Sunday.

From Durrus, you can turn off for the **Sheep's Head Peninsula** or continue straight on to Bantry, 10 km away. The Sheep's Head Peninsula is unspoiled and is less visited than many of the nearby areas. At **Ahakista** you can see Cork sculptor Ken Thompson's memorial to the 329 victims of an Air India plane crash off the coast in 1985.

The **Sheep's Head Way** is a waymarked walk around the peninsula that covers 90 km of low hills and rugged coastline. The walk is circular, starting in Bantry, and going out the

Dunmanus Bay

northern side of the peninsula to the lighthouse at its tip, then around the peninsula to Kilcrohane, Ahakista and Durrus, then back to Bantry.

Bantry and Glengarriff

If you are going directly from Cork to Bantry, it is slightly faster to go via Bandon, Dunmanway and Drimoleague, than through Skibbereen and Ballydehob. Bus Eireann goes the Dunmanway route. However, if you're driving and have time to spare, the southern route described above is more scenic.

Looking out on Bantry Bay and Whiddy Island and across to the Caha Mountains, **Bantry** is one of the bigger towns in West Cork. While once it relied mainly on sea fishing, it is now a busy tourist centre, especially during the summer months.

In 1689, a French fleet attempted entering the bay to help James II in his fight against the Williamites but was forced to retreat. Over a century later, in 1796, Wolfe Tone and a French armada sailed into the bay with the aim of leading the United Irishmen in their attempt to overthrow British rule. However, severe weather conditions meant that less than half of the 15,000-strong troops arrived, and after failing to land, they returned to France.

Bantry House (Tel: (027) 50047), built in the late 1700s, is one of the main attractions. As you drive into Bantry from the east, you will see the sea on your left; and Bantry House is on the right-hand side of the road. It offers a stunning view over the blue waters of the bay. The Georgian mansion is perfectly preserved and is open to the public. The 45 acres of gardens are well-groomed and the interior of the house is opulently decorated with nineteenth-century furniture and paintings. Bantry House is also home to the 1796 French Armada

Bantry House

Exhibition Centre which outlines the story of the unsuccessful invasion. The house, gardens and Armada Exhibition are open from 17 March until October, 9 a.m.–6 p.m. Admission to the gardens and Armada Exhibition costs €4. See *www.bantryhouse.ie*.

Continue past Bantry House and you will arrive at the town's centre, Wolfe Tone Square. Bus Eireann buses will drop you off outside Murphy's Bar on the quays just before the square. A busy market takes place on Fridays in the square.

If you want to stay in the town, **Vickery's Inn** (Tel: (027) 50006) is a good option. It has been there since the early 1800s, and although it has had a few refurbishments since then, it retains some of the old charm. Rates are €35–€45 per person. The **Bantry Bay Hotel** (Tel: (027) 50062) is also right in the town and has rooms for €45 per person and single rooms for €55. The **Westlodge Hotel** (Tel: (027) 50760) is a large three-star hotel on the eastern edge of the town overlooking Bantry Bay. It is looking rather dated these days, but is well-equipped and family-friendly with a swimming pool, tennis court and children's playground. Bed & breakfast is from €65 per person sharing. There are also some three- and four-star self-catering cottages available.

For food, **O'Connor's Seafood Restaurant** on Wolfe Tone Square (Tel: (027) 50221) serves mussels, fresh lobster and plenty of other seafood varieties in atmospheric surroundings. There is also a good restaurant attached to the 1796 pub, while **The Brick Oven** (Tel: (027) 52500) on Wolfe Tone Square serves tasty pizza at a reasonable price. **The Snug**, also on the square, is a good spot for decent, inexpensive pub grub. **Ma Murphy's** on New Street is a wonderful old pub with a small grocery store at the front and a beer garden out the back, while the **Anchor Bar** on the same street is a lively enough spot for a few drinks.

Bantry Mussel Fair

Mussels are big business in Bantry and the **Bantry Mussel Fair** takes place every May, when a stage is set up in Wolfe Tone Square with free live events. While the line up on the main stage is often not too exciting, the town's pubs tend to be teeming as hundreds of visitors descend on them. There are plenty of mussels to be had as well. For line up info, log on to *www.bantrymusselfair.ie*.

A little more reserved is the **West Cork Chamber Music Festival** that takes place at Bantry House over 10 days in July. It draws soloists and quartets from all over Europe and beyond. For programme information, Tel: (027) 52788 or look up *www.westcorkmusic.ie*.

On the twenty-minute drive from Bantry to Glengarriff, stop off at one of the viewing points to get panoramic views of Bantry Bay. The small village of **Glengarriff** is more green and lush than the surrounding areas. It is a tourist hot spot and can be a little twee, packed with tourist shops selling leprechauns and overpriced woolly jumpers to the tour buses that pass through. The surrounding landscape is spectacular though, with the Caha Mountains towering over the sheltered bay.

You will spot the main tourist office (Tel: (027) 63084) on the main street. It is a good spot to stop off for some walking, as the nearby forest offers plenty of good pathways of varying difficulty. The ten-minute boat trip to the wooded **Garnish Island** is also worthwhile for the stunning views of the surrounding mountains from the beautifully sculpted gardens on the island. It is a horticulturalist's paradise, with exotic flowers from all over the world, but even those who don't know anything about gardening will appreciate the colours and beauty when the garden is in bloom. From the boat, you may even spot some seals on the warm rocks. From Glengarriff, the journey to Kenmare in County Kerry is breathtaking, with a tunnelled road cutting through the Caha Mountains.

Italian Gardens, Garnish Island

The Beara Peninsula

The other road out of Glengarriff leads to the wild landscapes of the remote **Beara Peninsula**, part of which is in County Kerry, the rest is part of Cork. The 48-km-long peninsula tends to be much less clustered with tourists than nearby destinations, especially outside the summer months. The unforgiving landscape of the Beara is pretty barren, but has a haunting beauty, encompassing the Slieve Miskish

Mountains, a few sandy beaches and rocky islands.

The Beara Way Walking Route covers over 200 km of tracks, old roads and mountain paths and offers spectacular, unspoilt scenery. It is one of the best spots in the country for walks. There is an adjacent cycle route as well that covers more than 130 km. Pick up a free guide to walking and cycling in the area from Cork Kerry Tourism.

The first stop is the village of **Adrigole**. The village itself does not have much going on but there are some nice beaches nearby and plenty on offer for anyone who can sail or wants to learn. The **West Cork Sailing and Powerboating Centre** (Tel: (027) 60132) at the Boathouse in Adrigole provides sailing and powerboating holidays and training courses. It is possible to sign up for residential courses with accommodation and meals for two days or more. Course-only options are also available.

Beyond Adrigole is **Hungry Hill**. There is a lake on top of the hill, and when this overflows, it creates one of the country's highest waterfalls. The hill provided the setting for Daphne du Maurier's novel, *Hungry Hill*. The book was also made into a feature film of the same name.

If you continue west along the road past Adrigole, you will arrive at **Castletownbere**, a large fishing port at the foot of Hungry Hill, overlooking, and sheltered by, Bere Island. The town is home to one of the largest fishing fleets in the country and plenty of foreign trawlers pass through here.

Although not the prettiest of West Cork's towns, it's a good starting point for daytrips up to Hungry Hill or across to the Bere Island, and is also a good spot to eat, drink and withdraw money with the only ATM on the peninsula. The town caters well for tourists but its residents do not rely on tourism; fishing is the main source of income. As a result, Castletownbere does not have that almost fake feeling that some of the more touristy towns and villages in West Cork can sometimes have.

Beara Tourism and Development Association (Tel: (027) 70054) is located in the main square, and also has a good website at *www.bearatourism.com*.

Watersports fans would be well advised to check out **Sea Kayaking West Cork** (Tel: (027) 70692), run by Frank Conroy from the town. There are half day, or one, two or three day options, exploring the waters of Bantry Bay to the south of Castletownbere, and no experience is necessary. For more information, look up *www.seakayakingwestcork.com*.

The windswept landscapes of Beara attract artists from all over, and **Mill Cove Gallery** (Tel: (027) 70393) in Castletownbere is a good place to check out some of their work. For a sneak preview, log on to *www.millcovegallery.com*. The **Sarah Walker Gallery** (Tel: (027) 70387) in the town is also worth a look. The **Beara Arts Festival** takes place around the end of July/beginning of August and most of the action centres around Castletownbere.

It is in Castletownbere that you will find **McCarthy's Bar** made famous by Pete McCarthy's book of the same name.

Two car ferries leave for **Bere Island** several times a day (more often in summer than in winter). The island has some quiet, sandy beaches, and a couple of pubs.

If you leave Castletownbere and continue west again for a couple of kilometres you will come across **Dunboy Castle** which was burnt out in 1921. In the grounds are the remains of the original castle that was destroyed at the start of the seventeenth century.

Continue west to the tip of the peninsula where you will see **Dursey Island**, which can be reached by Ireland's only cable car. The island, which has only a handful of inhabitants, is a haven for bird watchers. The two-hour walk along the track leads to spectacular cliffs at the far side of the island.

Back on the mainland, the road that rings the peninsula leads around to **Allihies**, a pretty village that has lost much of its charm due to the number of holiday homes built around it. However, there is no denying the beauty of its setting, with glacial mountains on one side, the sea on the other.

In the 1800s, Allihies was a prosperous copper-mining town and the now defunct mine shafts are still visible. In fact the white sand of the beach at Ballydonegan isn't real sand at all, but ground-up sand that was used for mining.

Allihies has a couple of shops and four pubs, **O'Neills, O'Sullivans, The Lighthouse** and **The Oak Bar**. O'Neills is probably the best for food and is often the liveliest. A few miles outside Allihies is a tin roof pub where Christy Moore was known to drop by and sing a few songs from time to time. He is less likely to do so now though, as he refuses to perform in places where alcohol is served.

Further along the ring road, to the north of the peninsula is **Eyeries**, which is quieter and less spoiled by holiday homes

Eyeries, Beara Peninsula

(above and below) Healy Pass

than Allihies. It is set slightly inland but still has views of the sea. About 8 km west of Eyeries is the **Anam Cara Writer's and Artist's Retreat** (Tel: (027) 74448) which provides residential facilities for artists wishing to spend some time in the area. Further along the northern coast again is an even smaller village, Ardgroom. Between Eyeries and Ardgroom, you can stop off to see Ireland's tallest Ogham stone. Further along the same road is the famous Hag of Beara.

The next village after Ardgroom is Lauragh which is over the Kerry border. At Lauragh, take a right turn to return to Adrigole via the Healy Pass. The road cuts right through the mountains and offers breathtaking scenery as you descend towards Bantry Bay.

10 THE CORK GAELTACHT

Macroom

Macroom provides a gateway to the Cork Gaeltacht, the area of Cork where the Irish language is spoken. West of Macroom, the Gaeltacht encompasses Ballyvourney, Coolea, Inchigeela and Ballingeary. Further to the south-west, the island of Cape Clear is also a Gaeltacht (see Chapter 9).

Macroom is situated about 35 km west of Cork where the Lee and Sullane rivers meet. It is a large and busy market town built over a 10-arched bridge on the main Cork–Killarney road. The thirteenth-century Macroom Castle was burnt down in 1922 during the War of Independence. All that remains are the **Castle Gates** which can be seen right in the centre of the town. The castle was once occupied by William Penn, the founder of Pennsylvania.

The **Castle Hotel** is near the Castle Gates (Tel: (026) 41074) and has been extensively refurbished recently, with an excellent leisure centre. The Victoria Hotel (Tel: (026) 41082) on the square is also right in the centre of town and has a good reputation. It offers good value with rooms from €35 per person sharing. **The Auld Triangle** pub (Tel: (026) 41940) on the western edge of Macroom has excellent bar food.

Ballymakeera, Ballyvourney and Coolea

When you drive west from Macroom, the road gets narrower and more windy and the landscape becomes more rocky and rugged as you enter the Cork Gaeltacht. After about 10 km, you will arrive at **Ballymakeera**, a long village that stretches for about a mile and then becomes **Ballyvourney**, a continuation of the village. It is on the main Cork–Killarney road so plenty of tourists stop off there on their way to Kerry. If you turn left at the Mills Inn at Ballyvourney and cross the bridge, the winding road will take you through the hills of **Coolea**, with the village itself recognizable by the church.

St Gobnait is the patron saint of this area. She founded a convent here in the sixth century, and the site still draws pilgrimages. As well as being a Gaeltacht, the area has a strong musical and literary heritage. The famous writers Seán Ó Ríordáin and Seán Dunne are buried here. The composer Seán Ó Riada spent much of his life in Coolea and his son Peadar, also an accomplished musician, still lives here and plays regularly. Seán Ó Riada was largely responsible for the popular revival of Irish traditional music and his mass, which put old Irish-language prayers to the music of the area, is famous all over the country. Coolea's choir, Cor Chúil Aodha, is often in demand around the country and abroad but the best place to hear them is on their own turf, led by Peadar Ó Riada, at the 10 a.m. mass in Coolea.

At the beginning of each December, a weekend-long festival of music and singing, known as **Éigse Dhiarmuidín Ó Shúilleabháin**, takes place around the pubs of Ballyvourney and Coolea. It is always extremely busy during this weekend as people travel from all over and it is certainly necessary to book ahead.

The Cultural and Heritage Centre (Ionad Cultúrtha Baile Mhuirne) in Ballyvourney holds traditional music concerts on the first Friday of every month, except for July and August. The centre also holds educational programmes. For more information, Tel: (026) 45733.

The rolling green hills that rise up on either side of Ballyvourney make the area popular with hillwalkers.

There are plenty of places to stay around the area. **The Mills Inn** in Ballyvourney has been around since 1775 and it is reputed that Daniel O'Connell used to stop off here on his way to Kerry. The grounds are beautiful, with the ruins of a sixteenth-century tower in the garden. The rooms are adequate and the restaurant is excellent. It is a popular drinking spot as well, with live music several nights a week. Room rates are from €44 per person sharing. A few doors down, the **Abbey Hotel** (Tel: (026) 45324) is a small, comfortable hotel with a restaurant and lounge bar. It is reasonably priced.

In Ballyvourney, **An Crúiscín Lán** is a small roadside café serving fresh homemade produce. Back in Ballymakeera, **O'Connell's** pub has barely changed at all in forty years. While it may not be to everyone's taste, it's a great place to stop for a good pint of plain and a chat with the locals. Its proprietor, Maire O'Connell, always gives a warm welcome. There are a few more pubs scattered along the road that makes up Ballymakeera and Ballyvourney. In Coolea, the tiny pub called **Top of Coomb** claims to be the highest pub in Ireland, and is well worth a trip into the hills, although you may not always find it open.

Ballingeary and Gougane Barra

The drive from Coolea to **Gougane Barra** offers some dramatic scenery as the road cuts through and climbs over the rocky, gorse-covered hills and wild moorland. To get to Gougane Barra, you must pass through **Ballingeary**, also a Gaeltacht village. During summer, the village plays host to hoardes of teenagers sent to the Gaeltacht to practise their Irish. In nearby **Inchigeela**, the Daniel Corkery Summer School, which usually takes place in July, caters for older Irish language enthusiasts with classes in Irish poetry.

Less than a kilometre from Ballingeary is the entrance to the national park at Gougane Barra at the source of the River Lee. There is a tranquil lake surrounded by wooded hills belonging to the Sheehy and Derrynasaggart mountain ranges. In the middle of the lake is an island on which a small church stands.

Gougane Barra

It is here that St Fin Barre had his hermitage in the sixth century before he travelled to what is now Cork city to set up a monastery there. You can walk across to the island. There are a number of different forest walks of varying length and difficulty. If you are at all fit, the extra exertion for the steeper, more difficult climbs will be well rewarded with stunning views of the glacial valley.

> *There is a green island in lone Gougane Barra*
> *Where Allua of songs rushes forth as an arrow;*
> *In deep-vallied Desmond – a thousand wild fountains*
> *Come down to that lake, from their home in the mountains.*

(Gougane Barra – JJ Callanan)

The **Gougane Barra Hotel** (Tel: (026) 47069), overlooking the lake, has been in the same family for several generations and is in a magnificent setting. Its bar and restaurant do good business from daytrippers in need of refreshment after exploring the park. Room rates start at €60 per person sharing.

11 NORTH COUNTY CORK

The inland area to the north of the county is not nearly as touristy as the coastal areas of East and West Cork. The landscape is much tamer in this part of the county as you travel north to the Blackwater Valley and then on towards the rich farming land that is known as the Golden Vale. North Cork is not without its attractions however, and if it's fishing or horseriding you're interested in, you need look no further than the Blackwater Valley. There are plenty of castles and old country estates that date back a few centuries. Many of them are in ruins today. This part of Cork is known for its rich literary heritage. The sixteenth-century poet, Edmund Spenser, lived in Doneraile for the best part of twenty years, while Elizabeth Bowen, William Trevor, Canon Sheehan and Thomas MacDonagh are all names that are associated with the area.

Fermoy

The first major town you'll come across when you take the Dublin road out of Cork is **Fermoy**, 30 km from the city. As you approach Fermoy, you will see the wooded **Corrin Hill** to your left, on top of which is a cross. The hill overlooks Fermoy Golf Club. Take a left off the main road and following the signs for the golf club, you will come across the entrance to the woods. The walk to the top of the hill is pleasant and not too taxing.

Fermoy itself is a busy town situated on the Blackwater River and both the Dublin–Cork and Rosslare–Killarney routes pass through it. If you turn left at the main square, and then left again before the bridge, and keep walking away from the bridge, the road turns into a small riverside path that offers a peaceful setting for a riverside walk. Rowing is a very popular activity in the town, and you will often see crews on the river. Fishing is the other popular pastime, with trout, salmon and coarse fishing on the Blackwater and Funshion rivers, but if you are not interested in angling, there really is not too much reason to stop here.

If you do decide to stop though, check out the **Grand Hotel** (Tel: (025) 31865) on the waterfront. Having been left derelict for a number of years, it has recently been restored to its former splendour. The bedrooms at the front of the hotel offer nice views of the bridge and the Blackwater, as does the bar. At lunchtime there is a good carvery, while in the evenings, there is a small bistro and a less expensive dining room offering à la carte and table d'hôte options.

Further outside the town, **Castlehyde Hotel** (Tel: (025) 31865) is a beautifully restored eighteenth-century country house and courtyard in secluded woodland by the Blackwater River. Single rooms go from €110 with doubles from €140 (prices are a little lower in low season). The restaurant, though expensive, has a very good reputation and is in a wonderful setting. Nearby Castlehyde House is owned by Michael Flatley of Riverdance fame.

La Bigoudenne at 28 MacCurtain Street (Tel: (025) 32832) is a lovely little restaurant run by a French couple serving authentic French cuisine in unpretentious surroundings.

Fermoy to Mitchelstown

From Fermoy, you can go east towards Lismore in County Waterford, which is a very pleasant journey. Otherwise, if you cross over the bridge and keep driving north, you will be back on the main Cork–Dublin road. The next major town along this road is Mitchelstown, but before reaching it, there are a few detours worth taking.

One such detour is to the village of **Glanworth**, with its fifteenth-century thirteen-arch bridge. You will see the ruins of a twelfth-century castle sitting on a clifftop, and beneath it an old mill that has been converted into a guest house, **Glanworth Mill** (Tel: (025) 38555). Each bedroom is decorated according to the themes of different local writers, for example the Edmund Spenser room for Elizabethan grandeur, the Alice Taylor room for country style. There are two good restaurants in the Mill, the informal Mill Room and the more formal Old Bridge Restaurant.

From Glanworth, you can continue on to **Ballyhooly**, where you will find what remains of the fourteenth-century Ballyhooly Castle, and further along the same road is **Castletownroche**, with 'The Old Rustic Mill by the Bridge' as the nineteenth-century song goes. If you continue further along the road again, you will eventually arrive at Mallow (see below).

Back on the Fermoy–Mitchelstown road, there is another turn-off to the left for **Kildorrery**, about 10 km off the main road. Another kilometre or so past Kildorrery is the site which was once the home of the famous novelist, Elizabeth Bowen (1899–1973) and is the subject of one of her most famous works, *Bowen's Court*. Bowen is buried in the nearby churchyard. Further along the same road, you will come across a signpost for **Doneraile**. Doneraile Court once belonged to Edmund Spenser, before being sold to the St Leger family. The house is now owned by the Irish government, and the 400 acres of wooded, landscaped parkland, complete with Irish red deer, are open to the public. Open daily 11–sunset, admission is free. Spenser lived at **Kilcolman Castle**, a short drive from here, for a number of years in the late-1500s and it was here that he wrote his best-known work, *The Faerie Queene*. Spenser held extremist views of the native Irish people and how they should be dealt with, and as a result, the castle was attacked and burned out by rebels in 1598. Spenser and his wife survived but their infant son died in the fire. All that is left now of the castle is the ivy-covered tower perched on a small hill, but there are good views of the nearby Ballyhoura mountains.

Back on the main road again, and **Mitchelstown** is only a couple of kilometres further on. It is a market town in the middle of the Golden Vale, surrounded by rich farming land. Despite good views of the nearby Galtee mountain range, the town itself has little to warrant stopping for any length of time. The annual **Mitchelstown Music Festival** takes place over the August Bank Holiday weekend (first weekend in August). An outdoor stage is set up in the town square for free live music, usually consisting of Irish pop acts, and the bars play host to different types of music too.

Mallow

It is possible to go from Mitchelstown to Mallow via Kildorrery, but the more direct route from Cork is to follow the Limerick road. **Mallow** is a thirty-minute drive from the city, and buses run every hour from 7.25 a.m. to 7.25 p.m. (take the Limerick bus). The town is instantly recognizable by the large blue sugar refinery that dominates the townscape. It sits on the River Blackwater and so is popular with anglers.

The tourist office is on Bridge Street (Tel: (022) 42222) next to the gates of Mallow Castle. The first castle was constructed here in 1185, and in 1585 a new one was built on the same site. The ruined sixteenth-century castle is a National Monument, and is open to the public. It is in the grounds of a newer castle that is privately owned and is not accessible to the public.

The nearby half-timber **Clock House** was built in Tudor style in 1855. During that century, it was used by the 'Old Rakes of Mallow Club', a notorious group of gamblers, drinkers and hunters. Nowadays, things are less exciting inside the building; the ground floor houses an accountants office.

Another Tudor-style building is the **Spa House** which dates back to 1828. Out the back is a large well known as Lady's Well. The building once housed medicinal baths. It is now used as an Energy Agency office.

About one and a half kilometres west of Mallow stands the ruined sixteenth-century **Dromaneen Castle** which looks directly across the Blackwater River at **Longueville House**, built in 1720. Longueville (Tel: (022) 47156), on its 500 acres of grounds, is now a twenty-bedroomed old-style hotel that also has a very good restaurant. A room there can set you back from €95 to €360 per night.

Springfort Hall Hotel (Tel: (022) 21278) is a large eighteenth-century country manor hotel about 6 km outside Mallow in the direction of Doneraile. It has comfortable rooms and a good restaurant with a set dinner menu for €40.

Mallow is not served well for restaurants, but **O'Callaghans** at 83 Main Street (Tel: (022) 20922) is a cut above the rest and has a good early bird between 5.30 p.m. and 7.30 p.m.

Less than 2 km outside Mallow, **Cork Racecourse** (Tel: (022) 50210) is the premier venue for horseracing in County Cork. It was completely refurbished a few years ago. Admission is usually about €15, and a race card costs €2.50. Corporate packages and suites are also available. To find out fixtures and times, look up *www.corkracecourse.ie*.

At the main roundabout at Mallow, you can go west towards Kanturk or north along the Limerick road to Buttevant and Charleville.

Kanturk is a small, well-kept town situated where the rivers Allow and Dalua meet. Of the many ruined castles in the area, **Kanturk Castle** is the finest and is well worth a visit. It was built in 1601 by a MacCarthy chieftain, but the castle was never fully completed after British settlers complained and London ordered that the building be stopped. The four-storeyed rectangular building has a large tower at each corner, and still has fireplaces on the interior.

If you choose to go north from Mallow, another fifteen minutes down the Limerick road is the smaller town of **Buttevant**, which was once a walled town owned by the Anglo-Norman Barry family. It is surrounded by old ruins, and a river runs through the town, although you won't see it from the main street. Just before you get to Buttevant, you will pass the ruins of **Ballybeg Abbey**, an Augustinian abbey founded in the thirteenth century. Popular legend has it that the name of the town came from the term 'Boutez-en-avant' (push forward) used by the Barry family. It is more likely, however, that the name came from the Norman-French word botavant, meaning defensive fortress. The first steeplechase from the steeple of the Protestant church here to the (now gone) steeple at Doneraile, 7 km away, took place in 1752. The Cahirmee Horse Fair, an old-fashioned horse fair that has been going on for centuries, takes place in the middle of July.

12 EAST CORK

The coastline east of Cork stretches as far as the seaside town of Youghal, about 50 km from the city, on the Waterford border. Despite the fact that there are plenty of good, sandy beaches and attractive villages, this coastline does not tend to be as visited by tourists as that of West Cork.

Midleton

A short drive from Cork city, Midleton is a busy market town that is growing rapidly due to the increasing commuter population. Its main tourist attraction is the **Jameson Distillery** which still has a fully operational water wheel from the nineteenth century, along with a number of other historical features. Tours of the distillery finish up with a whiskey-tasting session. From March to October, tours take place from 10 a.m. to 6 p.m. with the last tour beginning at 4.30. Between November and February, three daily tours are scheduled at 11.30, 2.30 and 4 p.m. For more information, Tel: (021) 461 3594 or check out *www.whiskeytours.ie*.

If all that whiskey makes you hungry, the **Farm Gate** on Broderick Street (Tel: (021) 463 2771) is owned by the same people as its namesake in the English Market in Cork and the standard is just as good, with fresh, local produce being the order of the day. It is open daily from 9 a.m. to 5.30 p.m., and also opens for dinner from Thursday to Saturday, 7 p.m.–9.30 p.m.

Jameson Distillery, Midleton

Raymonds on Distillery Road (Tel: (021) 463 5235) has a varied menu ranging from roast beef to Thai fishcakes and does a very good value early bird menu for €22. **Finin's Restaurant & Bar** on Main Street (Tel: (021) 463 1878) has expensive but very good bar food. **McDaids** on Main Street is a good spot for live music and draws a young crowd.

Cloyne and Shanagarry

Cloyne is a small cathedral village about five miles south of Midleton. St Colman founded his monastery here in the sixth century, and there is a thirteenth-century cathedral but it is not in great condition. **Cross of Cloyne** Restaurant (Tel: (021) 465 2401) draws people out from the city as well as from the Cloyne area. It is open Wed–Sat, 6 p.m.–9.30 p.m., Sundays 4 p.m.–9.30 p.m. **Barnabrow Country House** just outside Cloyne (Tel: (021) 465 2534) offers wonderful, country house accommodation in an informal atmosphere. Rooms are available in the main house or in a courtyard and each room is tastefully decorated in its own individual style. The **Trinity Rooms** restaurant is housed in a large old hall with a high ceilings, wooden beams and long banquet tables. See pictures of it at *www.barnabrowhouse.ie*.

If you continue through Cloyne towards **Shanagarry**, you will see a sign for **Ballymaloe House** (Tel: (021) 465 2531), a fifteenth-century manor that houses one of the best-known restaurants in Ireland as well as a luxurious country house hotel. Lunch is €25 per head and the five-course dinner will set you back €55 and is worth a splurge if you can afford it. Ballymaloe is also well known for its cookery courses, which are very popular. For information about the restaurant and hotel, see *www.ballymaloe.com*.

For information about the cookery courses, check out *www.cookingisfun.ie*.

You will also see signs in Shanagarry directing you to **Stephen Pearce Pottery** (Tel: (021) 464 6807) which is well worth a visit. As well as buying some hand-painted, hand-decorated pottery, you can watch the potters in action carrying on a 250-year-old tradition in this part of the country. Stephen Pearce is open seven days a week, 10 a.m.–6 p.m. *www.stephenpearce.com*.

Ballycotton

Just past Shanagarry is Garryvoe, a blue flag beach that can get very busy on summer days. If you go back to Shanagarry and follow the signposts for **Ballycotton**, you will arrive at the

Ballycotton

pretty fishing village after about three miles. There is a clifftop walk that offers stunning views of Ballycotton Island (now a bird sanctuary) and the nearby lighthouse. The **Bayview Hotel** (Tel: (021) 464 6746) is a four-star hotel situated on a clifftop overlooking the harbour. A room will set you back from €129 a night, but if that's too steep, it's worth a visit for Sunday lunch in luxurious surroundings or for a drink at the bar while taking in the view. Bar food is served daily, 1 p.m.–5.30 p.m. and dinner is served every night, 7 p.m.–9 p.m. Spanish Point Restaurant (Tel: (021) 464 6177) has its own fishing trawler and naturally specializes in fresh seafood. The **Grapefruit Moon Restaurant** (Tel: (021) 464 6646) also has a very good reputation and is open Wed–Sun from 7 p.m. Across the road, **The Blackbird Pub** regularly sees local musicians jamming and has an excellent programme of live events.

On the road between Ballycotton and Aghada, be careful not to blink or you'll miss the crossroads village of **Ballinrostig**. It consists of a handful of houses, a quaint church and a pub called **Walls**. With an open fire, good stout and a cosy atmosphere, Walls is a gem of a pub and provides a perfect spot to while away a winter's Sunday.

Youghal

Further east, next to the Waterford border, is the seaside town of **Youghal**. The town's history dates back to the ninth century, and it has been designated an Irish Heritage Port. Lying on a narrow stretch of land with the sea on one side and hills on the other, the town has several kilometres of sandy beaches around it. In its heyday, it was a popular seaside resort, with the amusement arcades and good beaches drawing the crowds. It was used as the location for the filming of John

Clock Gate, Youghal

Huston's *Moby Dick* (memorabilia of which can be seen in the bar of the same name). These days, the town is a little run down but still has plenty which to charm its visitors.

Occupied first by the Danes, and then by the Normans, Youghal was a prosperous trading port from medieval times. In 1275, Edward I oversaw the building of a wall around the town. In the sixteenth century, the town was allocated to Sir Walter Raleigh, who sold it to Sir Richard Boyle, Earl of Cork, in 1602. Boyle is buried in St Mary's Church.

The tourist office (Tel: (024) 20170) is located in Market Square, not far from the **Clock Gate**. Enquire about the walking tour that leaves from the tourist office. There is a good heritage centre joined on to the tourist office that traces the town's history back to the ninth century.

The narrow main street that runs from one end of the town to the other is crossed by Youghal's most famous landmark, the Clock Gate, which was built in 1777 on the site of an earlier town gate. The Georgian tower crosses the main street with an arch underneath through which traffic flows. It was used originally as a prison. From the tower, there are steps up a steep narrow hill to the top of the town where some of the medieval walls can still be seen.

On Church Street, the thirteenth-century St Mary's Collegiate Church is built into the town's walls and is one of the oldest churches still in use. It incorporates elements that date back as far as the tenth century. Next to it is Myrtle Grove, where Sir Walter Raleigh lived in the late 1500s while he was mayor of Youghal. Unfortunately, the house, one of the oldest unfortified houses in the country, is privately owned and no longer open to the public.

The busking festival in August is a good time to walk around the town, taking in the sights and listening to music on the streets at the same time.

Old walls, Youghal

Aherne's Hotel & Seafood Restaurant on 163 North Main Street (Tel: (024) 92424) has been in the Aherne family for several generations. There are nice rooms and apartments to stay in and the restaurant is well known for its excellent seafood. If you're on a budget, the bar food is good too and the bar tends to have a good atmosphere. **The Old Imperial Hotel** at 16 North Main Street (Tel: (024) 92435) dates back to the eighteenth century. It has good rooms for about €50 per person and a very good restaurant, **The Coach House Restaurant**.

Hostel accommodation near the beach is available at **Evergreen House**, The Strand (Tel: (024) 92577). Dorm beds cost €13 while a double room costs €36. A few hundred metres away is **Tides Restaurant** (Tel: (024) 93127) which does good seafood dishes and has comfortable accommodation.

INDEX

Page numbers in italic refer to illustrations